Hiking with Ghosts

From every social rank, across the continent and beyond, thousands came to seek their fortune in Klondike gold.

Hiking with Ghosts

The Chilkoot Trail

Frances Backhouse
Photographs by Adrian Dorst

RAINCOAST BOOKS

Vancouver

First published in 1999 by

Raincoast Books
8680 Cambie Street
Vancouver, B.C.
V6P 6M9
(604) 323-7100

www.raincoast.com

1 2 3 4 5 6 7 8 9 10

CANADIAN CATALOGUING IN PUBLICATION DATA

Backhouse, Frances
    Hiking with Ghosts

        (Raincoast journeys)
        ISBN 1-55192-276-8

    1.   Backhouse, Frances—Journeys—Chilkoot Trail. 2. Chilkoot Trail—History.
          3. Chilkoot Trail—Description and travel. I. Dorst, Adrian. II. Title. III. Series.
          FC4045.C45B32 1999   971.9'1   C99-910497-7
          F1095.K5B32 19999

Editing by PaperTrail Publishing
Interior design by Metaform Communication Design

Raincoast Books gratefully acknowledges the support of the Government of Canada, through the Book Publishing Industry Development Program, the Canada Council and the Department of Canadian Heritage. We also acknowledge the assistance of the Province of British Columbia, through the British Columbia Arts Council.

PRINTED IN ITALY

Table of Contents

CHILKOOT TRAIL

World's Longest Museum

Overloaded, and frantic to reach the goldfields, the stampeders in 1897-98 abandoned gear all along the trail. Hiking in their footsteps you may spy stoves, cookware and shoes half-buried among the rocks.

The historic litter has value and meaning only if left in place along the gold rush trail. Please do not disturb the artifacts (they are protected by Federal, State, and Provincial laws).

Cheechakos: Greenhorns

As ill-equipped goldseekers struggled up the trail, old-timers called them Cheechakos, a Tlingit word for greenhorn.

It took the average stampeder 3 to 4 weeks to pack his "ton of goods" from tidewater (Dyea) to Lake Lindeman. Your load may be lighter, but you face some of the same hazards. Weather can be extreme, especially on Chilkoot Pass. Start this hike only if prepared for severe conditions.

◄●►

Le musée le plus long du monde

En 1897 et en 1898, les chercheurs d'or, surchargés et pressés d'atteindre les gisements aurifères, ont laissé du matériel le long du sentier. En suivant leurs traces, vous apercevrez peut-être des poêles, des articles de cuisine et des chaussures à demi enterrés sous les roches.

Ces artefacts n'ont de valeur que si on les laisse à leur place le long du sentier de la ruée vers l'or. Ne les déplacez pas (ils sont protégés par la loi, au Canada comme en Alaska).

Cheechakos: les débutants

Les chercheurs d'or mal équipés qui gravissaient péniblement le sentier se faisaient appeler "Cheechakos" par les plus expérimentés, mot qui signifie débutant en langue tlingit.

Il fallait de trois à quatre semaines au voyageur moyen pour transporter sa "tonne de biens" du chenal de Dyea au lac Lindeman. Votre charge est peut-être moins lourde, mais vous devrez tout de même affronter quelques-uns des dangers qui guettaient les chercheurs d'or. Le temps peut se faire très violent, surtout dans le col Chilkoot. N'entreprenez cette randonnée que si vous êtes prêt à affronter des conditions difficiles.

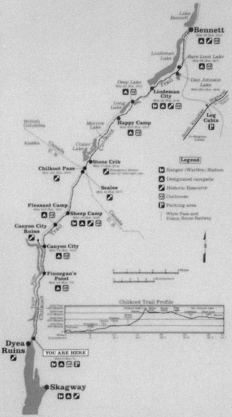

Map labels

Lake Bennett
Bennett
Lindeman Lake
Bare Loon Lake
Deep Lake
Dan Johnson Lake
Lindeman City
Long Lake
Log Cabin
Morrow Lake
Happy Camp
British Columbia
Alaska / Canada
Crater Lake
Stone Crib
Chilkoot Pass
Scales
Pleasant Camp
Sheep Camp
Canyon City Ruins
Canyon City
Finnegan's Point
Dyea Ruins
YOU ARE HERE
Skagway

Legend

- Ranger (Warden) Station
- Designated campsite
- Historic Resource
- Outhouse
- Parking area
- White Pass and Yukon Route Railway

Chilkoot Trail Profile

Acknowledgements

I WOULD LIKE TO OFFER MY THANKS TO THE PEOPLE WHO ASSISTED ME IN gathering information about the Chilkoot Trail for this book. First and foremost is Karl Gurke, cultural resource specialist for Klondike Gold Rush National Historical Park, who has welcomed me to Skagway on several occasions and was singularly obliging when it came to answering questions and providing feedback as I was writing this book. Karl also introduced me to two other very helpful United States National Park Service employees, seasonal archaeologist Eve Griffin and botanist Claudia Rector. On the other side of the border, I received assistance from Dan Verhalle, Laura James, David Neufeld and Bob Lewis, all of Parks Canada. JoAnne Nelson and several of her colleagues at the British Columbia Ministry of Energy and Mines provided additional information, as did Syd Cannings of the British Columbia Ministry of Environment. While I appreciate all the assistance these individuals offered, I accept full responsibility for any informational errors that may have slipped in despite their best efforts.

On behalf of all three of us who made this trip, I also offer thanks to the White Pass and Yukon Route railway and Canadian Airlines for generously helping to offset some of the costs of travelling to and from the trail, and to Carol Smith of Whitehorse for providing exceptional hospitality at both ends of the trip.

My final and greatest debt of gratitude goes to Mark Zuehlke for his companionship, enthusiasm, wise counsel and loving support.

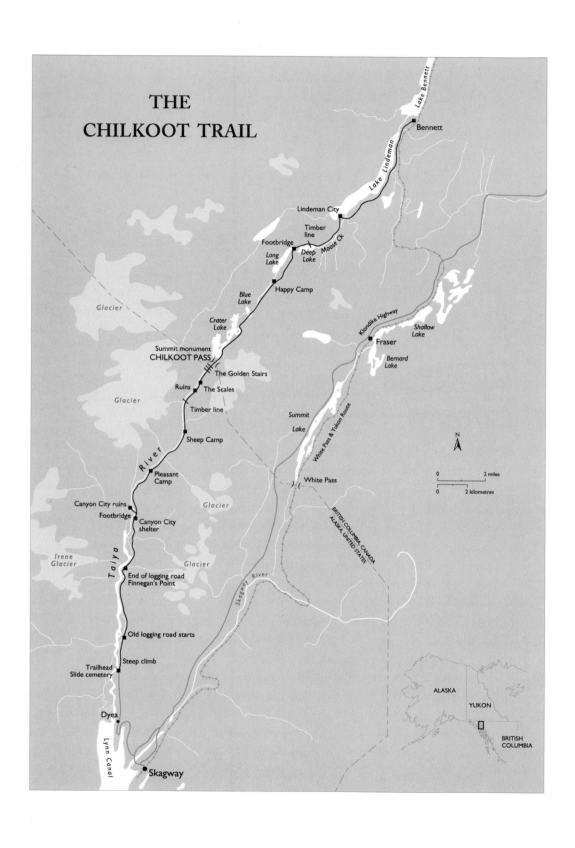

THE
CHILKOOT TRAIL

Lake Bennett

Bennett

Lake Lindeman

Lindeman City

Timber
line

Moose Ck

Footbridge

*Long
Lake*

*Deep
Lake*

Happy Camp

*Blue
Lake*

*Crater
Lake*

Klondike Highway

*Shallow
Lake*

Fraser

Summit monument
CHILKOOT PASS

*Bernard
Lake*

The Golden Stairs

Ruins   The Scales

Glacier

Timber line

*Summit
Lake*

Glacier

Sheep Camp

White Pass & Yukon Route

Pleasant
Camp

Canyon City ruins

Glacier

White Pass

Footbridge

Canyon City
shelter

*Irene
Glacier*

Glacier

End of logging road
Finnegan's Point

Taiya

Skagway River

River

Old logging road starts

Steep climb

BRITISH COLUMBIA CANADA
ALASKA UNITED STATES

Trailhead
Slide cemetery

N

| 0 | | 2 miles |
| 0 | | 2 kilometres |

Dyea

ALASKA

YUKON

Lynn Canal

Skagway

BRITISH
COLUMBIA

Prologue

THE CHILKOOT TRAIL HAS GONE THROUGH MANY INCARNATIONS. ORIGINALLY it was a trade route used by members of the First Nations of Alaska, northern British Columbia and the Yukon, long before those place names ever appeared on maps. Later it was travelled by non-Native prospectors on their way to and from the northern interior. It became internationally renowned during the final three years of the 19th century, when 30,000 to 50,000 fortune seekers used it to gain access to the headwaters of the Yukon River and, ultimately, to the Klondike goldfields. Then it was abandoned, left to return to nature.

The modern Chilkoot Trail, which began to emerge in the 1960s, is a world-class backpacking route managed jointly by the United States National Park Service and Parks Canada. On August 15, 1998, the Canadian and American governments officially designated the Chilkoot Trail as part of Klondike Gold Rush International Historic Park, along with other gold-rush sites, including Dawson City in the Yukon and Klondike Gold Rush Historical Park in Seattle, Washington.

Many people are drawn to the Chilkoot Trail because of its fascinating past, but to infer that it is only of historical interest is to underestimate its other attractions. The Chilkoot corridor is magnificently scenic and biologically diverse. The 53-kilometre route provides a unique opportunity to travel by foot through three distinct ecosystems — coastal rainforest, alpine tundra and boreal

forest. The trail also offers a challenging backcountry experience in the rugged terrain of the Coast Mountains, an adventure often made additionally challenging by severe weather conditions. It is not a trip for the unfit or the ill-prepared.

In 1998, a century after the peak year of the Klondike stampede, nearly 4,000 people hiked the length of the Chilkoot Trail. I was one of them. This book is the outcome of that trip and a previous excursion that I made in 1994, while researching a book about the women of the Klondike gold rush. Like the braided Taiya River, which parallels the southern half of the trail, my narrative has many strands. By intertwining history, landscape, flora and fauna with an account of my two journeys, I hope to present a portrait of the trail that will spark memories for others who have hiked it, inspire future Chilkoot trekkers and entertain armchair travellers who have the good sense not to go climbing mountains in the pouring rain.

The Chilkoot Trail begins at sea level near the mouth of the Taiya River, 15 kilometres northwest of Skagway, Alaska. It runs straight north for about 13 kilometres, then continues in a northeasterly direction for the rest of its length. The highest point on the trail, the 1,122-metre-high Chilkoot Pass, is almost exactly halfway between the two ends. This summit also represents the boundary between the United States and Canada. The ghost town of Bennett, British Columbia, where the trail ends, lies at about 650 metres above sea level. Modern backpackers have the choice of walking 13 kilometres from Bennett out to the nearest road or returning to civilization by boat or train.

The most famous, and the most dreaded, portion of the Chilkoot Trail has always been the nearly 45-degree ascent that became known during the Klondike era as the Golden Stairs. The lead-up to this section consists of a stiff six-kilometre climb up 530 metres from Sheep Camp to the Scales, the area where commercial packers used to weigh their loads and calculate their fees. The rocky stairway to the summit begins just beyond the Scales and rises nearly 300 metres over a mere 900-metre distance.

People looking at a map of the Chilkoot Trail for the first time are occasionally confused by the fact that its northern terminus is in British Columbia. "Weren't the stampeders on their way to the Yukon?" they ask. Indeed they were, but the Chilkoot Trail was only one leg of a long journey that also included a great deal of water travel. An ocean voyage of about one week's duration brought the gold seekers from West Coast ports like Seattle and Vancouver to the beginning of the trail. Then, when they reached the end of the trail, they embarked on an 800-kilometre expedition down the Yukon River, from its headwaters at Bennett to Dawson, deep in the heart of the northern interior.

Short as the Chilkoot Trail was in relation to the overall distance the Klondike stampeders travelled, it took most of them weeks or months to traverse and it left an indelible imprint on their memories. Even without a ton of goods to transport, I found this trail had a similar impact on me.

Introduction

IN APRIL, WINTER STILL RULES ALASKA AND THE YUKON. ALTHOUGH THE DAYS are rapidly lengthening and the heat of the sun can once more be felt, this remains a land of ice and snow. An uncompromising land that does not hesitate to punish those who do not understand or respect its ways. On April 3, 1898, winter handed out its harshest sentence to some five dozen people who, among all the thousands on the Chilkoot Trail that spring, had the misfortune of being in the wrong place at the wrong time. They have gone down in history as the victims of the Palm Sunday avalanches.

To those who were familiar with the land, there were plenty of warning signs of the impending disaster. First Nations packers who were working on the trail knew that a change in the weather had made the heavy snowpack unstable on the steep slopes around the Chilkoot Pass, and they refused to go up there. But many of the stampeders who were swarming across the Coast Mountains on their way to the Klondike were unwilling to pause in their mad pursuit of fortune. The folly of their decision became evident on the night of April 2, as great slabs of snow started peeling off the mountainsides in the vicinity of the pass and tumbling into the narrow Taiya Valley below. By morning, two separate slides had buried 23 people in the vicinity of the Scales, but others had managed to rescue them. The first deaths came a few hours later when two more avalanches entombed three people in their tent and obliterated a party of tramway workers

Modern-day tourism helps keep Skagway's past alive.

as they retreated from the danger zone. No lives were spared. Meanwhile, the last 200 people who had remained up at the Scales, hoping to avoid backtracking, had finally acknowledged the danger they faced there and had started down toward the treeline. Because blizzard conditions had reduced visibility to almost zero, the stampeders walked single file, clutching a long rope to keep from losing track of each other and the trail. Unaware of the fate of the tramway workers, they arrived at the place where that fatal slide had occurred only an hour or so earlier. As they approached, a second avalanche came hurtling down the mountainside, instantly burying those who were at the front of the rope and leaving their comrades at the rear untouched but stunned. Digging frantically, the survivors were able to save a few of the victims, but many perished. No one was ever sure of the exact number of those who died that day. Best estimates suggest the final toll was 65 to 70.

One hundred years later, on a warm, sunny August afternoon, I am thinking about these unfortunate souls as I stand in the small cemetery near Dyea, Alaska, where they were laid to rest. Simple wooden grave markers tilt at odd angles or lie prone, grey against the dark green leaves and scarlet fruit of the bunchberries that carpet the ground. Over and over again I read the same fateful date, but the inscriptions reveal little about the identities of those whose graves they mark. C. Beck – Sandford, Florida. J.C. Murphy – New York, N.Y. Mrs. A.U. Maxon – Pumzataney, P.A. Like most of the men and women who travelled the Chilkoot Trail during the height of the Klondike gold rush, the avalanche victims had left their families and friends at home and were travelling independently or with just a few companions. Within the mass of humanity that converged here at the end of the 19th century, the majority of the deceased were virtually anonymous. A few of the bodies were claimed by acquaintances, who paid to have them shipped back home. As for the rest, their fellow stampeders pieced together whatever information was available about them – from a name found on a letter in a pocket, perhaps, or from someone's recollection of a hometown mentioned in passing. They laid the corpses of the dead strangers in the ground, marked the graves and did what they could to notify the next of kin. Then they carried on.

The Palm Sunday tragedy caused a few stampeders to reconsider their plans, but most remained intent on getting to the Klondike. They knew they were taking a risk in venturing into the northern wilderness. Avalanches were just one of the hazards they faced. Death could as easily come by hypothermia, drowning or illness. Why did they do it? Well, obviously for the gold. For the chance to shake off the burden of poverty that so many carried during those years of worldwide economic depression. For the adventure and the thrill. These answers are no secret, but it's still hard to truly comprehend what motivated tens of thousands of individuals from all over North America and from every other continent to travel to this remote shore and face the challenges of such a gruelling journey without any guarantee of success.

Tidewater, Dyea: the start of the trail for 19th-century Chilkoot trekkers.

I know I am not alone in my desire to peer back into the hearts and minds of the stampeders. Almost every person I've talked to who has hiked the Chilkoot Trail has expressed similar thoughts. If the dead were with us still — the ones who died en route to the Klondike and the ones who lived to a ripe old age and never stopped telling stories about this most amazing time in their life — they might explain. Certainly they have left a wealth of written material that attempts to do so, but I have trouble hearing those voices properly when I'm lounging by the fire in my living room or sitting in the bright silence of an archives. I prefer casual conversation that lifts and lulls as I walk along. Stories inspired by a sight, a sound or a scent. And so, I am going to go hiking with ghosts.

I will begin at the Dyea townsite, the historical jumping-off point for Chilkoot Trail travellers. Although not an official part of the modern Chilkoot route, this is where the Klondike stampeders, and the Tlingits who originally established the trail, began their journeys. It is also where my hiking companion, Mark, and I have decided to begin ours. Adrian, the photographer assigned to this expedition by the publisher, has opted to skip Dyea and get straight onto the trail, so we will catch up with him later.

Dyea is located 15 kilometres west of Skagway at the head of the Lynn Canal. Travelling north along the coast of British Columbia and Alaska, this long, narrow fjord draws the Inside Passage to a close. Dyea was first settled by the coastal

Ant-like, in an unbroken line, men packed their heavy loads up the precipitous slope to the summit.

Tlingit people as one of their most northerly villages. They used it as a base for making trading forays up the Taiya Valley and across the Coast Mountains into the northern interior. Europeans began visiting and passing through Dyea in the late 1700s. The first Europeans to explore the Lynn Canal were the British under Captain George Vancouver, who named the waterway after King's Lynn, his home in Norfolk, England. Russian, American and British fur traders arrived soon after Vancouver and were followed in turn by a small but steady trickle of prospectors.

The first non-Native to settle in Dyea was John J. Healey, an American who had earlier co-founded Fort Whoop-Up in southern Alberta, one of the most notorious whiskey-trading posts in the West. At Fort Whoop-Up he had built his profits around deceitfully plying the Blackfoot with a vile whiskey substitute made from ingredients like tobacco, molasses and red ink, which sometimes killed those who drank it. Healey's Dyea trading post, established with partner Edgar Wilson in 1884-85, was a more honest operation. Nevertheless, his attempts to elbow the Tlingits out of the fur-trading business and to turn the Chilkoot Trail into a toll road suggest that he still had little respect for First Nations citizens. Until the summer of 1897, this quiet community consisted primarily of a collection of Tlingit homes and the Healey and Wilson store. Then all hell broke loose.

One of the peculiarities of the Klondike gold rush is the way northern geography caused it to develop in two distinct phases. When Keish (Skookum Jim Mason), Káa Goox (Dawson Charlie) and George Carmack discovered gold on Bonanza Creek in 1896, it was already mid-August and the chill of autumn was in the air. Although news of their find spread like wildfire throughout the North in the following weeks, freeze-up came too soon for word to get out beyond the Yukon and Alaska. Not until two boatloads of gold-laden miners landed in San Francisco and Seattle the following July did the rest of the world learn about this natural treasure trove. It did not take long for the thousands who were instantly infected with Klondike fever to realize that the quickest and least expensive route to the goldfields was over the Chilkoot and the White Pass Trails. Practically overnight, Skagway — the jumping-off point for the White Pass route — exploded into existence, and the small Native village at the foot of the Chilkoot Trail metamorphosed into a thriving metropolis.

By the fall of 1897, the Dyea townsite had been laid out in neat blocks, and buildings were being thrown up with breath-taking speed. Dozens of hotels, restaurants, saloons and retail stores lined the streets. Doctors, lawyers and seamstresses hung out their shingles wherever they could find space. There was no shortage of customers. During the winter of 1897-98, 30,000 to 40,000 people passed through Dyea, and the town's transient population peaked in late winter at about 8,000.

Dyea today could not even be called a ghost town. Time and the forces of nature have very nearly erased it from view. A tour of the site is an exercise in imagination and is enhanced by a knowledgeable escort, so we have decided to delay our departure and go on one of the Dyea "bushwacks" offered by the U.S. National Park Service four days a week.

In Skagway, our point of departure, our inquiries about transportation to Dyea lead us to a robust man with a bushy blond mustache who goes by the name of Dyea Dave. Early in the afternoon we meet our chauffeur outside the Trail Center at the foot of Skagway's crowded Broadway Street. Mark and I climb into his van along with six others who have signed up for the bushwack. We soon learn that Dave is a local who makes his living showing tourists the nearby sights and conveying hikers to and from the Chilkoot Trail. He is both knowledgeable and loquacious, and he regales us with stories as he drives. He also stops for a quick viewing of the Dyea cemetery, which is too far from the main part of the town to be included in the Park Service tour. At the appointed hour, Dave turns us over to our guide, Matthias Matt.

The tour begins with Matthias leading us out onto a flat, grassy expanse that stretches south toward the ocean, where lofty mountains flank the Lynn Canal and appear to converge in the far distance. In springtime, these meadows are blue with wild irises. Now they are decorated with pink fireweed and ivory-toned yarrow. Here and there, young Sitka spruce trees stand stiffly among the languid grasses and flowers. Stopping beside what appear to be a couple of weathered stumps, Matthias draws our attention to a line of similar stumps extending all the way to the water's edge. These are the remains of pilings, he tells us. Originally they supported a pier known as Long Wharf, because of its incredible 3.2-kilometre span.

From the placement of the pilings it would appear that much of this wharf was built over dry ground, but such is not the case. One hundred years ago, these meadows were muddy tidal flats that were submerged for half the day and exposed for the other half. Dyea was an awkward location for a port because the tidal flats prevented ships from getting close enough to shore to conveniently unload freight and passengers. Water deep enough to accommodate large vessels was nearly two kilometres from the high-tide line. People who disembarked when the tide was out had to struggle through the muck to get all their gear moved to higher ground before the ocean flowed back in and washed it away. The completion of Long Wharf in the spring of 1898 solved this access problem.

Even if Dyea had survived beyond the gold rush, this wharf would have eventually become obsolete because the entire Taiya Valley, including the mud-flats into which the pilings were driven, was and still is rising out of the ocean at a rate of two centimetres per year. During the Pleistocene ice age, the weight of the glaciers that covered this land caused the pliant subcrustal rock beneath them to deform and flow, slowly but surely, away from the ice accumulation centres. When the ice melted, it was as if a very heavy person had gotten out of bed, leaving

Past and present coexist — the ghosts are beginning to gather.

"Man's best friend" had real meaning on the arduous Chilkoot Trail.

a sag in the mattress. Gradually the subcrustal rock has been flowing back and the sag has been disappearing as the land lifts. Because of this phenomenon, known as isostatic rebound or post-glacial uplift, Dyea is now two metres higher than it was 100 years ago and the mudflats are now meadows.

This is not the only change that time has wrought. A forest of Sitka spruce and cottonwoods has also taken over most of the townsite. As we walk along, Matthias points out subtle clues to the past: a rectangle of sunken vegetation that indicates an old cellar; a straight line of trees marking the edge of a street. Not one single intact structure remains, and the only upright remnant is the false front of a building that once stood on the southwest corner of Fifth Avenue and Main Street. I find it delightfully ironic that this lone survivor was once the A. M. Gregg real estate office, where Mr. Gregg no doubt declaimed his visions of Dyea's glorious future to all who stepped inside.

When developments elsewhere caused the Chilkoot Trail to fall from favour as a transportation route, Dyea went bust as quickly as it had boomed. One reason so little of the town remains is that many of the buildings were shipped out, whole or in pieces, to Skagway and other communities along the Alaska coast.

The other reason is that the town was built along the west bank of the Taiya River's main branch, and over the past century that channel has shifted, washing away a significant portion of the old business district.

Matthias leads us up Broadway, now just a mossy trail, until we reach a crumbling riverbank and can go no further. "In 1898," he says, "this street we're walking on was the beginning of the Chilkoot Trail." I borrow his copy of an old townsite map and trace the route — from the waterfront to the northern edge of town at Seventh Avenue, just beyond where we are now standing, then on through the military reservation, the Native village, and the secondary commercial district known as Uptown or North Dyea. From there, the stampeders crossed a bridge over the Taiya and strode off into the wilderness. Gazing north up the valley, I feel impatient to follow them.

After answering a few final questions, Matthias winds up the tour just after 3:00 p.m. and leads us back to the parking lot, where Dyea Dave is waiting. It takes only a few minutes for him to deliver us to the modern-day trailhead on the east side of the Taiya River. Just before Dave drives off, we ask him to take a photograph for us — the "before" picture, with bodies, hair and clothes fresh and clean. Mark, who has just shaved off his beard for the first time in decades, looks more boyish than his 42 years, and his pack sits easily on his broad shoulders. Judging by the comments of Dyea Dave's other passengers, who are watching from the van, I'm looking a little scrawny in comparison to my partner, despite my months of working out in preparation for this trip. The picture taken, Dave and the others wish us luck. We wave good-bye as the van pulls out of the dusty parking lot. I do a few warm-up stretches, then we turn toward the trees. This is it. The Chilkoot Trail.

Trailhead to Finnegan's Point

THE CHILKOOT IS NOT A TRAIL THAT LETS YOU EASE GENTLY INTO YOUR HIKE. No sooner have we left the parking lot than we are climbing a steep, rock-studded, root-tangled prominence known as Saintly Hill. As the sweat trickles down my ribs and my heart starts to pound, I think about the real climb — the Golden Stairs — two days away. Should I turn back right now? But having survived the trail once before, I am not really worried. I know that beyond this initiation, the rest of the eight-kilometre leg to Finnegan's Point is quite moderate.

After heading straight up for about 400 metres, the trail levels off and we stop to catch our breath, already happy to relieve ourselves of the unaccustomed weight of our packs. This morning when we left our Skagway hotel, Mark and I figured they weighed about 21 and 19 kilograms, respectively, but at the top of Saintly Hill they seem to weigh twice as much. After our pulses return to normal, we start our descent toward the Taiya River. We will be following its course all the way to Sheep Camp, though often the water will be out of sight and earshot. The first convergence of trail and river comes just beyond the foot of Saintly Hill, and when we get there I can't resist stopping for a few minutes to admire the view west across the wide valley to the distant, jagged mountains.

The river is that translucent, milky colour peculiar to all glacier-fed waterways, with their burden of rock that has been ground to a fine powder by ice. In the shallows where the water is clearer, metallic-looking flecks glint in the sun.

Views of the Taiya River, such as this, are timeless, no different today than a century ago.

From the start, the trail plunges into lush coastal rainforest.

Even knowing they are only tiny chips of mica, I am momentarily enthralled by the fantasy of dipping a pan into the river and swirling it until I am left with a few spoonfuls of precious gold dust. If I had been alive back in 1897, would I have been among the thousands of foolish dreamers who were stricken with gold fever? I'd like to think not, but I can't deny the way my eyes were drawn to every Skagway storefront window that featured a display of shiny flakes and nuggets. Lillian Oliver, a young Chicago housewife who made a solo journey to Dawson in 1898, later described the compulsion that drove her. "I dreamed of rich finds," she wrote in *Wide World Magazine* upon her return, "and bags of gold haunted me all day and at night troubled my rest." Perhaps I would have been similarly obsessed.

Certainly, had I acted on that obsession, I would have had little chance of fulfilling my expectations. By the time word of the strike reached the outside world, every decent claim in the Klondike district had been staked by people who were already in the North when the gold rush started. Except for a few rare individuals who were just plain lucky, the only people who got rich were shrewd mining speculators and hard-working entrepreneurs. Some of the latter never even bothered crossing the Coast Mountains, since there was plenty of money to be made meeting the needs of the stampeders on this side of the pass.

Back on the trail, we cross several streams running into the Taiya. We pause on the bridges and look for spawning salmon. They should be here at this time of year, but if they are, the murky water is keeping them hidden. The consolation prize is a pair of mergansers resting on a half-submerged log. The sharp-billed birds regard us with wary interest before launching themselves into the current.

Now that the trail has connected with an old logging road and become wide and flat, we settle into a comfortable pace. As I walk, I reach out periodically and sample a tart, juicy highbush cranberry — *kachich* to the Chilkoot Tlingits, for whom the month we call August was "berry picking" time and September was more specifically "cranberry picking" time. The crimson fruit is refreshing and grows at an ideal height for snacking on-the-go. The cranberry bushes are part of a thick understorey that includes goatsbeard, devil's club, red-osier dogwood, ferns, mosses and low-growing herbaceous plants like clasping twisted stalk and one-sided wintergreen. They are shaded by a forest of tall, fast-growing black cottonwoods and shorter, more spindly Sitka spruce that have not yet reached their full size. Here, as elsewhere along the trail, there are few old-growth trees. Farther up the valley, many were felled during the gold rush for fuel or building materials, or burnt in forest fires started by careless stampeders. South of Finnegan's Point, they mostly survived the stampede only to be logged out during the 1950s.

The lush greenery along this stretch of the trail is typical temperate rainforest, encouraged by the wet and relatively mild coastal climate. Moist air from above the ocean is blown inland and cools as it rises over the mountains, causing much of the water vapour to condense and fall as rain or snow. While not as wet as some parts of the Alaska Panhandle, Dyea receives a generous 1,270 to 1,520 millimetres of precipitation annually. Temperatures on the windward side of the mountains are influenced year-round by the Japan Current, which holds the ocean at about four degrees Celsius and moderates the temperature of the overlying air.

The Taiya Valley's plentiful vegetation supports an abundant and diverse wildlife population, and provides plenty of cover for animals of all sizes to hide from human intruders. Our senses tuned to bears, we note frequent evidence of their presence: large footprints in the wet sand of river's side channels; dark, berry-filled scats, which we examine in passing to determine their freshness; pockets of musky scent that remind me of the summer I once spent tracking grizzlies on the north coast of British Columbia. Not a glimpse of the big beasts themselves, however. The only mammal we see during our first day of hiking is a vole, which Mark spots sitting on a decaying stump. While it plays peek-a-boo with us for several minutes, popping in and out of holes in the stump, I try to decide whether it has the characteristic "peppery" colouring and long whiskers that would identify it as *Clethrionomys rutilis dawsoni*, Dawson's northern red-backed vole, a subspecies named after geologist and explorer George M. Dawson, who passed this way in 1887.

Dawson's journey came less than a decade after the Tlingits had begun allowing non-Natives to use this trail, one of several traditional trading routes between their coastal territory and the interior. For many generations, the Tlingits had travelled back and forth across the mountains to exchange goods with the interior Athapaskan First Nations, including the Tutchone and Tagish. From the shores of the Pacific, the Tlingits brought eulachon grease, spruce root baskets, cedar boxes, fungus for red paint, dried clams, seaweed, abalone shells and obsidian. They returned home with mountain goat wool, tanned caribou and moose hides, furs, wolf lichen for yellow dye, porcupine quillwork and copper. This trade was beneficial to both sides, and there was respect and sometimes intermarriage between the two groups. Nevertheless, the Tlingits were the controlling partners. Their dominance was reinforced in the second half of the 18th century when Russian fur traders with an insatiable appetite for sea otter pelts arrived on the coast.

Around the end of the 18th century, a rapid decline in sea otter populations due to overhunting caused the traders to shift their attention to other sources of fur, such as marten, beaver, lynx and wolverine. The cold winters of the northern interior produced superior furs, and the Tlingits readily moved into the role of middlemen, acquiring pelts from the inland groups and transporting them to the coast, where they offered them to the Russian, British and American traders in exchange for goods such as iron or steel axes, knives and traps, brass kettles, scissors, guns, blankets and glass beads.

Three of the five main trails that linked the coast and the upper Yukon basin originated at the head of the Lynn Canal. (The other two followed the Taku River to the south and the Tatshenshini River to the north.) The three routes linked to the Lynn Canal are known as the Chilkoot, the White Pass and the Chilkat Trails, the latter connecting present-day Klukwan, Alaska, to Kusawa Lake in the Yukon.

Each of these trade routes was controlled by a specific clan. On the coastal side, the Chilkoot Trail was controlled by the Crow or Raven (†ukàxh.àdi) clan of the Chilkoot Tlingits. The name Chilkoot, applied to this regional subgroup, was a corruption of the name of their main village (†khùt), located near present-day Haines, Alaska. Dyea was one of this group's other villages. The words Taiya (pronounced "tie-ya") and Dyea ("die-ee") are phonetic variations on the original Tlingit toponym, which meant "packing place."

What we now refer to as the Chilkoot Pass, the Tlingits called A Shakî, meaning simply "over it." Their neighbours on the inland side, the Tagish, called it Kwatese, which is variously translated as "over it" or "over the mountain." Until the time of the Klondike gold rush, English speakers generally referred to it as the Dyea Pass, although Lieutenant Frederick Schwatka of the United States Army mapped it as Perrier Pass in 1883.

Differences in names aside, until the late 1800s it was accepted by Natives and non-Natives alike that use of the Chilkoot Trail was the prerogative of members of the controlling clan and that anyone else who wanted to traverse it had to request permission from the clan's chief. The first white man allowed to use the trail was a prospector named George Holt, who travelled from Dyea to the Yukon's Marsh Lake in the spring of 1878 and returned by the same route in the fall. Wary of his intentions and determined to protect their commercial interests, the Tlingits insisted he be accompanied by guides who ensured he did not engage in any trade. Two years later, the Chilkoots granted trail access for the first time to a large group of prospectors, but only after insisting that each member of the party sign a pledge promising to refrain from all trading activity while in the interior.

Unfortunately for the Tlingits, growing outside interest in the mineral resources of the North kept bringing greater numbers of outsiders into the region. In response to mounting pressure to open the trail to all, the Tlingits agreed to allow non-Natives free access in exchange for a guarantee that they would hire Tlingits as packers and pay them fair wages.

For a short time, all was well, but the level of friction increased as the demand for packers began to exceed the Chilkoots' capacity. A U.S. government census conducted in 1880 estimated that the combined population of the Chilkats and Chilkoots was only 988. A decade later their population had fallen to 812, as European diseases continued to take their toll. Even with women and children packing during the busy spring season, there was more work than this small group could handle, and as the lucrative packing business drew competitors from other areas, conflicts between locals and outsiders became common. The Chilkoots also clashed with prospectors who figured one Indian was the same as the next and simply hired whoever was available.

Modern accounts often seem to suggest that greed was the primary motivating force behind the Chilkoots' attempts to monopolize the local packing business. This was probably also the prevailing view at the time, but one contemporary observer, U.S. Navy lieutenant and amateur anthropologist George Emmons, expressed a different perspective in a letter to a northern newspaper in 1886. As he explained to readers of the Sitka *Alaskan*, there were three reasons why the clan wanted to prevent others from packing on the Chilkoot Trail: it was their land; they had the best qualifications for the work, having been trained for this type of activity from an early age by carrying a light pack every day for a few hours; and they were liable if anyone was injured on the trail. This was demonstrated in 1887 when a Taku River Tlingit man accidentally fell and broke his leg while packing on the Chilkoot Trail. Under Native law the Chilkoots were held responsible for the mishap because it occurred on their territory, and they were required to pay compensation to the man's relatives to settle the affair.

Despite the logic of these arguments, when things eventually came to a head, the U.S. authorities in the region declared that the Chilkoots must give up their monopoly on the packing business. Typically, they backed up this edict with the threat of armed enforcement, and the Chilkoots acquiesced. By 1887, when George Dawson and his Geological Survey of Canada expedition came through, there were even a few non-Native packers working on the Chilkoot Trail.

From the moment the first wave of Klondike stampeders hit Dyea in late July 1897, the packing business flourished and rates rose accordingly. In 1883, Lieutenant Schwatka had paid $9 to $12 per 100 pounds (45 kilograms) to have his party's supplies conveyed from Dyea to Bennett. At the height of the gold rush, packers commonly demanded, and received, a dollar a pound for the same distance. The amount of weight transported by professional packers was often impressive. Schwatka was astounded that his First Nations packers, men who

Among the few to profit from the Trail were local Tlingit packers, like the ones at lower left and at lower right,
who carried provisions for fortune seekers.

Moss and lichen reclaim the forest, obscuring traces of the past.

weighed on average only 63 kilograms, could carry packs weighing more than 45 kilograms. Others noted that Native women and adolescents regularly carried 20 to 35 kilograms, with the women occasionally toting their infants as well.

A few packers performed feats of strength so incredible that they became legendary. Skookum Jim Mason, for example, earned his nickname by shouldering unbelievably heavy burdens during his days as a packer. Skookum meant "strong" in the Chinook trading language commonly used along the north Pacific coast at the time and was a fitting title for a man who thought nothing of hefting a 90-kilogram load over the Chilkoot Pass. Today, those of us who hike the Chilkoot Trail have no choice but to carry our own packs. Strangely enough, we do this as a form of recreation. Along this flat stretch between the trailhead and Finnegan's Point it doesn't seem like such a bad idea, but I'm not sure I'll still be thinking this way when I'm halfway up the infamous pass.

After our encounter with the vole we pass through an area where industrious beavers have caused minor flooding. The trail is muddy, but not as wet as it obviously was earlier in the season. Park maintenance crews have done what they can to make things easier by laying down logs in the worst sections. This is just the first of many examples we will encounter of the commendable efforts of the trail crews on both sides of the border. All the bridges — more than 20 of them on the American side — are in excellent shape, and the trail itself is in good repair despite being trodden by thousands of pairs of feet every summer.

Back in the gold-rush days there were a few private attempts to improve and maintain sections of the Chilkoot and White Pass Trails. Finnegan's Point, where we are headed, was one such venture. Near here, Dan Finnegan and his two sons built a bridge and a corduroy road, made of logs laid down crosswise, and attempted to charge users a $2 toll. They briefly succeeded, but as the number of people passing by each day increased from dozens to hundreds, they found themselves unable to compel the majority of them to pay up. George Brackett encountered a similar situation on the White Pass Trail when he built a wagon road and tried to impose a fee of $40 for every ton of freight hauled over it. Unlike Finnegan, however, Brackett profited handsomely from his enterprise once he managed to enlist the backing of the U.S. Army, which brought the defiant stampeders in line.

Not only do modern hikers enjoy the benefits of a well-maintained trail, they also avoid some of the challenges the stampeders faced. The original route followed the course of the Taiya for about 13 kilometres, until the wide river valley narrowed dramatically at a spot that became the site of Canyon City. Winter travel was relatively easy, but once the ice melted there was no way to avoid numerous crossings of the river's braided channels, only a few of which were served by ferries or spanned by bridges. Lillian Oliver, the Chicago housewife who dreamed of bags of gold, wrote that the river had intersected her path 14 times between Dyea and Canyon City. She crossed it once on a makeshift bridge created by a fallen tree, four times by wading through the icy water, and the other nine times was carried across by her loyal guide.

Besides being inconvenient, the river could also be hazardous, as the Holmes party discovered in August 1897. This group of five men and one woman had set off from Dyea dragging their flat-bottomed scow behind them. They were soon up to their knees in water, and then to their waists. When the channel started getting even deeper, they decided to try to cross to the other shore. Mary Holmes and two of the men climbed into the unwieldy boat. The others held onto the towline and tried to ease them across the river, but as the scow moved out into the current, the rope was wrenched from their hands. Suddenly the heavily laden vessel and its three passengers were speeding down-stream toward a treacherous log jam that had already been responsible for numerous wrecks and at least two deaths. They hit it broadside and the bow plunged into the water. To their companions, watching helplessly from the shore, it looked certain that the boat would fill with water and sink, but in the next moment a huge wave hit the stern, spinning the scow around and lodging it safely against the remnants of an old bridge. From there the shaken trio made it to shore with the boat. Undeterred by their mishap, they dried themselves and their gear and carried on.

No such excitement for us. Quite the opposite, in fact, for this part of the trail is almost tediously flat and easy. Finally, a slight uphill grade begins. At the top of the hill I spot a tall spruce that has a stubby wooden dowel of the type that would have once held a glass insulator nailed to it about five metres up. This is the first sign I have seen of the telephone line that once ran from Dyea to Bennett, at the end of the Chilkoot Trail, across to Log Cabin, near the White Pass summit, down to Skagway, and back to Dyea. In 1898, it was possible to make calls between any of these communities, most of which no longer even exist.

Not far beyond the telephone tree we come to a stream that, according to the U.S. Park Service's simple, two-page guide to points of interest, is a good place to fill our water bottles if we plan to stay overnight at Finnegan's Point. Unlike the milky Taiya River, the stream is clear. Nevertheless, we heed the warnings we have heard from several official sources to filter or treat all water obtained along the trail. Since we have not yet added a water filter to our collection of outdoor gear, I drop a tiny brown iodine tablet into each one-litre bottle. I think about wilderness guru Edward Abbey, who said, "When a man must be afraid to drink freely from his country's rivers and streams, that country is no longer fit to live in," but remind myself that those words were written back in 1968, when there were far fewer people travelling the backcountry and almost none of them had even heard of coliform bacteria or giardiasis.

At 6:00 p.m., about 800 metres past our water stop and two and a half hours after we left the trailhead, Finnegan's Point campground emerges out of

At "The Scales," each trekker's load was weighed to make sure it contained the requisite ton of supplies.

the trees. Other than the white canvas wall-tent that serves as a permanent cooking shelter, there are no other tents in sight. Adrian was planning to go as far as Canyon City today, and we have seen no one else on the trail except for a few day-hikers headed back to town. Unless there are any overnighters who left even later than us, it seems we will have the place to ourselves, a welcome prospect after the crowds in Skagway and the busy weeks leading up to this trip.

We choose a roomy tent site under a large spruce, not caring that it is right beside the trail, since we are not expecting much traffic. The river, which at this point runs close to the trail, is partially visible through the shrubs along the bank, but the beautiful Irene Glacier is hidden. To admire this river of ice flowing imperceptibly down the flank of Mount Yeatman on the far side of the Taiya, I have to walk down to the water's edge. The glacier is an enchanting turquoise colour — the result of the ice being so dense and so free of reflecting air bubbles that nearly all the colours of the light spectrum are absorbed and only the blue-green light waves are reflected. I consider taking Irene's photo, but she is already partially in shadow. I decide to wait until tomorrow, when the

morning sun will highlight the network of crevasses etched across her ancient face like wrinkles.

For dinner we have the heaviest of the seven evening meals we have packed: macaroni and cheese enhanced with sun-dried tomatoes and dehydrated green pepper. We also slice up half of the cucumber we harvested from our garden just before leaving and brought along, regardless of weight, for the sheer pleasure of eating something fresh. Meal planning for a backpacking trip is always a balancing act between bringing too much and too little. With this meal we erred on the side of excess, but we scrape the pot clean and force down every noodle. During the pre-trip lecture delivered to all hikers before they get their permits, the rangers prohibit dealing with leftovers by burning them, burying them or throwing them in the river. So given a choice between carrying them with us for the next week or stuffing ourselves now, we opt for the latter. I tell myself it's important to build up my reserves, in case I've also miscalculated in the chocolate department.

Just as I am finishing my last mouthful, Mark suddenly leans forward and points to something moving in the bushes about three metres away. Behind the dense foliage I see dark fur and instantly think "bear," only to realize a moment later that what I took to be the shoulder of a 200-kilogram grizzly is actually a 10-kilogram porcupine walking along a tree trunk bowed down close to the ground. Alarm is followed by relief and then fascination as we watch this shaggy creature make its way over to an upright birch, which it proceeds to climb, ponderously and with apparent disregard for our presence. Now that it is out in the open I can clearly see its black undercoat overlaid with long, creamy guard hairs and black-and-white banded quills.

In winter, porcupines must make do with a diet of bark and twigs, but come springtime they turn their attention to buds, leaves and catkins, often seeking the topmost branches in search of the most succulent new growth. A waddler on the ground, the "quill pig" is reputed to be a skilled tree climber, using its fleshy footpads and long, curved claws for traction and its muscular tail for extra support. This one strikes me as having a rather hesitant manner, yet it must possess its species' renowned sense of balance, for it carries on toward the highest limbs, while the trunk bends and sways under its weight. About the time Mark finishes doing the dishes, the porcupine finally stops and wedges itself into a crotch formed by a thin branch and the equally slender top of the trunk. In this precarious position it falls asleep and is still there when we retire around 9:00 p.m.

Full darkness has not yet descended at this point, although the sun's rays have long since retreated from the bottom of this high-walled valley. Even now, in the middle of August, the long days of the northern summer are still with us. I read for a short time in the gathering gloom, then give up and close my eyes.

Finnegan's Point to Sheep Camp

I SURFACE FROM SLEEP AT 8:15 A.M. LAST NIGHT THE SOUND OF THE RIVER WAS A soothing lullaby. This morning it brings me gently back from dreams. My body feels great after yesterday's easy, eight-kilometre warm-up, and I am looking forward to the next leg of the trip. Not even the sight of the heavily overcast sky that greets me when I emerge from the tent can dampen my spirits. With thick, grey clouds muffling everything above the 1,000-metre level, I won't be taking pictures of the Irene Glacier after all, but there is no rain and no wind, and I am delighted to be out here.

It is cool enough to warrant putting on pants and a long-sleeved shirt, but I don't mind since this protects most of my skin from the no-see-ums and mosquitoes that are prevalent here at Finnegan's Point. I apply a little insect repellent around my ears and neck like cheap perfume, then go off to retrieve our food bag from the bear pole, a simple structure consisting of two vertical supports and a horizontal crossbar that is well above the reach of both grizzlies and black bears. There is at least one bear pole at each of the nine designated campgrounds along the Chilkoot Trail, with the exception of Happy Camp, which has a bear-proof storage locker instead. Backpackers are under strict orders to keep all their food and garbage suspended from the poles at night and when not cooking or eating. This also goes for toothpaste, cough drops and any other potential temptations that might set a bear's nose twitching.

These trail-side birch provide a pleasant contrast from the usual grey-barked trees of the Chilkoot rainforest.

In addition to the bear poles, each of the sites on the American side and two of the five on the Canadian side (Happy Camp and Lindeman City) have cooking shelters, and those that don't have shelters have designated areas for cooking. All food preparation and eating is supposed to be confined to the shelters and their immediate vicinity or the designated areas, so that a clear distinction between sleeping areas and eating areas is maintained and any bears that are attracted by food smells will stay away from slumbering hikers. Thus far, all of the bears and most of the humans are behaving as intended.

The cooking shelter at Finnegan's Point — a standard design also used at Pleasant Camp and Sheep Camp — is a canvas tent stretched over a wooden frame. The platform on which the tent stands offers about 15 square metres of floor space. A tin-covered counter runs along the back wall, a bench extends the length of one side, and a cast-iron woodstove for warming the shelter stands opposite.

By the time I arrive from the bear pole, Mark has already lit our white-gas stove and put some water on to boil. Now to rummage through a week's worth of food to find coffee, milk powder and granola. Since we are the only campers here, we soon have supplies strewn all over the counter and the bench. As we discovered last night when we were cleaning up after dinner, this disorderly approach makes it easy for the local mice to chew holes in many plastic bags within a very short period of time, but our level of tidiness is not much better this morning. I decide the best defense is vigilance, and when we go outside to eat breakfast, we prop the tent's wooden door open and run back inside whenever we hear the sound of tiny, scuttling feet.

Despite not rushing through breakfast, we manage to pack up and get on our way by 10:00 a.m. Today's 12-kilometre hike to Sheep Camp will be our second longest haul on this trip. If we had been able to make an earlier start yesterday I would have preferred to spend our first night at Canyon City, as many people do, but I was not keen to follow the example of those who hike the entire 20 kilometres from the trailhead to Sheep Camp in one go. As a confirmed believer in a leisurely approach to recreation, I avoid covering that kind of distance when I'm carrying a full pack, if at all possible.

Almost as soon as we exit the campground, we leave the old logging road behind and the trail begins to ascend a long, gradual incline. As it did yesterday, the dense vegetation wraps us in its verdant embrace. Earlier in the season there would have been a scattering of multihued flowers among the omnipresent green of the understorey, but mid-August is almost autumn in this country. Now, before the leaves start turning yellow, red has its moment of glory in the form of highbush cranberries, bunchberries, baneberries, devil's club berries and *Amanita muscaria* mushrooms.

The ruddy, white-spotted Amanitas are not the only fungi bursting forth from the damp forest floor, but with their colouring and size — some are as big

Amanita muscaria mushroom thrives in the humidity.

as salad plates — they are by far the most dramatic. The consequences of eating these poisonous mushrooms are also dramatic, but they are not the most deadly plants out here. Of the many types of berries along the Chilkoot Trail, there is only one species that must be avoided. The baneberry's smooth, glossy, scarlet (or sometimes white) fruits look tempting, but eating as few as six berries can lead to vomiting, followed by bloody diarrhea and, finally, paralysis of the respiratory system.

About two kilometres past Finnegan's Point the trail joins an old riverbed, recognizable by the numerous small, rounded boulders strewn across the flat ground and a radical shift in vegetation. Beneath the sparse, spindly trees an exquisite array of lichens carpets the ground. Their subtle shades run from blue-grey to pale chartreuse to ash with just a hint of pink. The U.S. Park Service guide informs us that we have entered "the Rock Garden" and warns us not to trample the delicate, slow-growing plants, which are mostly members of the genus Cladina — the reindeer lichens. I crouch at the edge of the path and admire the intricately branched form of the nearest clump. It is eight centimetres tall and up close it resembles a dense, miniature forest of leafless oaks, whitened by hoarfrost.

The trail meanders across the old riverbed for nearly three kilometres, with the finest displays of lichens extending for about a quarter of that distance. In one section the trail has been cleared of rocks, some of which have been arranged along the sides of the trail as if it were a garden path. This is the work

of state prisoners brought here in the 1960s to build the American half of the recreational trail we follow today. By the time these work crews arrived, the original trail was already fading into the realm of myth and memory, and natural influences such as landslides and changes in the course of the river had made it impossible to restore the route exactly as it had been in the gold rush-era.

In 1898, with tens of thousands of people on the Chilkoot Trail, it must have seemed impossible that this pedestrian highway could ever disappear. Yet within months of the completion of the White Pass and Yukon Route railway between Skagway and Bennett in 1899, the Dyea-Bennett route was nearly deserted. The only people who continued to brave the Chilkoot Pass were the odd outbound prospector too broke to take the train and a few tradition-minded Tagish and Tlingit travellers.

Around 1915, members of the Skagway Alpine Club and other local residents began lobbying for the creation of a national park along the Chilkoot corridor. Unfortunately, the initial response from the decision makers in Washington was lukewarm. They admitted that the area had splendid scenery and abundant wildlife, but, in their opinion, the Taiya Valley was too littered with "junk" to be considered as a park. The fact that the junk (liquor bottles, boots, horseshoes, sled runners, cookstoves and the like) dated back to the Klondike gold rush was irrelevant. Eventually, in 1961, the government of Alaska stepped in and sent a group of delinquent teenage boys from a state detention centre to the area to begin reestablishing a trail to the summit. Trail-building and maintenance activities were continued by adult prisoners over the next seven summers and thereafter by government employees. No similar work was undertaken on the Canadian side of the border until 1968, when the first of several groups of inmates from the Yukon Correctional Institute was assigned the job of resurrecting the trail between the summit and Bennett Lake.

The U.S. National Park Service and Parks Canada set up their first ranger/warden stations, at Sheep Camp and Lindeman City, respectively, in 1973. Three years later, on June 30, 1976, the American president signed the bill that brought Klondike Gold Rush National Historical Park officially into existence. The Canadians were much slower to complete their paperwork. Even though Parks Canada was continuously active in the area from 1973 on, it was not until April 7, 1993, that Chilkoot Trail National Historic Site was formally established under the Canadian National Parks Act.

Most hikers are completely oblivious to this aspect of the trail's history — the dogged persistence of certain individuals who had a vision for this area; the mountains of memos now stuffed into file boxes and turning yellow in warehouses in Whitehorse, Juneau, Ottawa and Washington, D.C. There's no romance in bureaucracy, and besides, many of us simply take the presence of national parks for granted. Instead, every time we strap on our packs and head for the places cars can't go, we should salute the people who had the foresight to preserve these treasures for us.

After the Rock Garden, we plunge back into the forest, which looks even more lush after the dry, brittle beauty of the lichen landscape. We're still feeling fresh and the trail hasn't thrown anything too rough at us yet, so we make good time, arriving at Canyon City campground about 11:30 a.m. At the centre of the campground is a log cabin, where three young women who passed through Finnegan's Point while we were packing up this morning are relaxing on the porch. The chairs in which they are sitting are carved from sections of tree trunk that each measure nearly a metre across. They wave hello and ask us to take their picture. After Mark returns their camera, we exchange the usual trailside pleasantries and questions and are surprised to hear that they're planning to hike all the way from Sheep Camp to Lindeman City tomorrow. Although the distance is not much greater than that covered between the trailhead and Sheep Camp, the elevation gain to the top of the pass and the ruggedness of the terrain on both sides of the summit make this a challenging undertaking. At least one of them is starting to have doubts about their itinerary, but they all have to be back at their jobs in Skagway three days from now, so they are determined to succeed. I'm sure they will, being young and energetic.

The trio moves on and we take their places in the rustic chairs. Claiming note taker's privilege, I pick the one that is both an armchair and a rocker. It proves surprisingly comfortable and I settle in to record my impressions of the morning and to enjoy the view from the porch through the alders and cotton-woods to the flowing water and the hills beyond. It is with reluctance that I eventually rouse myself and go inside and look around the cabin, which is a legacy of the prison work crews. As part of their plan to avoid unpleasant encounters between bears and people, the Park Service has designated the cabin as a cooking shelter, and, like all the cooking shelters, it is not intended to be a place for sleeping or storing backpacks. Apparently, however, some people have not been paying attention to the 10-minute lecture on trail regulations and courtesies that we were all required to listen to before collecting our hiking permits at the Trail Center in Skagway. Pinned conspicuously beside the door there is a recent note that reads:

DO NOT STORE PACKS IN CABIN!!! I, PERSONALLY, HAVE SHOT AT A BEAR WHO WAS INSIDE THE CABIN. PLEASE HANG YOUR PACKS ON THE BEAR POLE.
— RANGER NANCY

Willful ignorance makes me cranky, especially in this case, when it can mean a death sentence for any bear that follows its instincts and yields to temptation. As we carry on down the trail I wonder whether the people who leave their packs in the cabin don't credit what the experts say about these animals' keen sense of smell or whether they simply believe they are above the rules that have been made to protect humans and bears alike.

In its lower reaches, the Taiya is a classic braided river with multiple channels winding back and forth across a wide, stony floodplain. Most early Chilkoot travellers — whether Native or not — took advantage of the flat, unforested valley bottom for the first leg of their upstream journey instead of fighting through the thick vegetation on the side hills. In winter they dragged their loads over the ice. In summer they piled their gear into canoes or scows. When the current was too strong for paddling they tied ropes to the vessels and pulled them upstream, hopping from gravel bar to gravel bar by wading through the water or using fallen trees as bridges. This comparatively easy valley-bottom route ends abruptly about halfway between Dyea and the Chilkoot summit, when the broad flood-plain is pinched closed by the high walls of a narrow canyon.

Like the Tlingit traders, who often camped at the mouth of the canyon, the Klondike stampeders saw this as a natural place to pause. From a nucleus of restaurants, roadhouses and other businesses set up by quick-thinking entrepreneurs at the dawn of the gold rush, Canyon City quickly grew into a bona fide town. Located on a large area of flat land on the west side of the river, there was plenty of room for expansion. By May 1898, streets had been surveyed and all the best lots had been snapped up. The community's shifting population of 1,500 lived in tents, cabins and the occasional frame house. Residents and travellers were served by at least 24 businesses, including hotels, restaurants, saloons, outfitting stores, barber shops, a doctor's office, a post office and a real estate office.

Like all the other Chilkoot Trail communities, Canyon City's lifespan was brief, though not as fleeting as some. Most residents left as soon as the railway became operational between Skagway and Bennett in July 1899, with a few staying on until early 1900. Rain, snow, salvagers and rampant regrowth have obliterated most of the town, but what is still visible is worth a look, even though it means making a short side trip.

To connect the modern recreational trail to old Canyon City, the prison work crews built a suspension bridge that spans the river about half a kilometre past the campground. In more recent times, a bear pole has been erected next to the bridge so backpackers can make the side trip unencumbered. Mark and I briefly consider taking advantage of this bear pole, but we're not sure our rope is strong enough to support the weight of our full packs, so we lug them with us.

We bounce across the bridge, then turn right and follow a path that runs along the riverbank through dense vegetation. We've been walking about five minutes when we meet the three young women again. They have made this side trip not knowing exactly what they might find and, seeing nothing of interest yet, have ended up turning back too soon. I tell them about an old stove up ahead that I found quite intriguing the last time I was here. They look at each other, weighing the dubious merit of retracing their steps against the burden of adding more distance to their already long day. "Maybe next time," one of them says with a shrug, and they continue in the direction of the bridge.

They've got a much heavier agenda than we do, I remind myself, and furthermore, not everyone gets a thrill out of seeing century-old flotsam and jetsam. After all, a few days ago when I mentioned to Adrian that I hoped he would take lots of photographs of artifacts along the way, he replied quite seriously,

Remnant of a grand scheme: this rusted hulk of a boiler remains from an aerial tramway
that hoisted Klondikers' loads up the pass.

"But who's really interested in rusty old buckets?" I started trying to explain the significance of such artifacts, but gave up when I realized that he hadn't really been looking for an answer.

When we come upon the stove less than 10 minutes later — shaded by a clump of alders, just as I recalled — it has the same effect on me as it had the first time I saw it. I imagine it standing in one corner of a low-ceilinged cabin, with a woman ladling beans from a large pot, being watched by a dozen ravenous men lined up on either side of a crude plank table. I imagine the smell of the hot apple pies she will pull from the oven in a few minutes when they have downed their beans and wiped their plates clean with thick slices of sourdough bread. I wonder what happened to all the men and women who warmed themselves by this stove, all those who satisfied their hunger with food prepared on and in it. For me, this trail is four-dimensional. It is relics like this that give it that extra dimension, that sense of existing in time as well as in space.

The stove, being large and solid, will probably be here well into the next century. Maybe the dented bread pans and other objects that have been piled on top of the stove will also remain, but I wouldn't count on it. When this trail was officially opened to hikers in the late 1960s, thousands of horseshoes and pieces of stampeders' gear were still scattered along the trail. One by one, they were picked up and carted home as souvenirs, leaving this outdoor museum stripped of many of its best artifacts, especially the smaller ones.

This apparently had a significant impact on the development of the trail. One of the objectives of the 1973 master plan for Klondike Gold Rush National Historical Park was to correct the mistakes made in laying out the recreational trail and reroute it to its original location where feasible. In their first few years on the job, National Park Service rangers discovered sections of the gold rush-era trail in the Canyon City area and between Pleasant Camp and Sheep Camp. But when they and the park's cultural resource specialists noticed that the quality and quantity of artifacts was significantly better along these remote stretches than along segments where the recreational right-of-way overlapped the historic trail, they lobbied vigorously, and successfully, against making changes that would allow modern hikers to walk more closely in the stampeders' footsteps.

Several hundred metres beyond the old stove, we find Canyon City's other major claim to fame: a huge boiler that once generated power for an aerial tramway (and lit up the town with the excess electricity). This tramway was part of a series of increasingly sophisticated freight transportation systems that were introduced along the trail before and during the gold-rush era.

For Klondike-bound travellers, the difficulty of getting their gear over the pass was one of the major drawbacks of the Chilkoot route. Horses were completely incapable of carrying loads up the steep grade of the Golden Stairs. Stampeders who had more time than money spent weeks moving their bags and boxes over the pass, piece by piece. Those with extra cash hired others to do the heavy labour, but unless they could hire a large contingent of packers, they still faced frustrating delays. It didn't take long for a few mechanically minded businessmen to see the potential for improving on this arrangement.

First off the mark was Juneau ferry operator Peter Peterson, who installed two different pulley systems at the pass before the Klondike gold rush even got going. His first, introduced in 1895, was a failure, but he returned the following year with a somewhat more successful version. It involved two wooden boxes, each attached to the end of the pulley rope. Freight was loaded into one box at the bottom of the incline, while the other box, at the top of the hill, was filled with snow. Then Peterson added his own weight to the upper box and rode it down the slope, pulling the freight uphill in the process.

The Chilkoot's first working tramway was contrived by Archie Burns. In the spring of 1897, he installed a wooden windlass at the base of the Golden Stairs and harnessed up a luckless horse that was forced to walk in an endless circle to drive the mechanism. By December, the one-horsepower windlass had been replaced by a gasoline engine and a drum pulley. Burns was purported to be able to move five tons a day up to the summit, but his achievements would soon be surpassed by the Dyea-Klondike Transportation Company, which had been formed in September 1897.

The Canyon City boiler was an integral component of DKT's plans for a transportation system that would extend from the beach at Dyea all the way to Lindeman Lake — plans that were hastily amended when it became evident two other companies were hot on their heels. Turning their attention to the pass, DKT managed to complete a two-bucket aerial tramway between the Scales and the summit by mid-March 1898. The buckets each held 225 kilograms and rode 90 metres above the ground as they made the round trip to the summit and back in 15 minutes. Since DKT's power source was back at Canyon City and the tramway was at the Scales, they had to link these two points with 13 kilometres of electrical power line strung from wooden poles.

One of DKT's rivals was the Alaska Railroad and Transportation Company, an arm of the Pacific Coast Steamship Company. By late April, AR&T had its system up and running. It began three kilometres above Sheep Camp and used a gasoline-powered engine to move an endless progression of smaller buckets, each capable of carrying 45 kilograms.

Meanwhile, the Chilkoot Railroad and Transport Company had figured out a way to run aerial freight cars all the way from Canyon City to the far side of the summit, just above the shores of Crater Lake. CR&T's operation employed two boilers — one at Canyon City, the other at Sheep Camp — and 72 kilometres of cable supported on tall wooden tripods. The cable was divided into two long loops, and an automatic switching mechanism at Sheep Camp transferred the cars from one loop to the next. The cars moved up the line at a rate of one per minute, at times soaring to heights of more than 500 metres above the ground. In one of her letters home to her husband in Chicago, Lillian Oliver mentioned that "after leaving Canyon City the Aerial Railway was with us over the tops of the trees and it was a strange sight to look up and see a cook-stove, a bale of hay, a canoe, lumber and other strange things flying by in the baskets in mid-air."

DKT charged five cents a pound to move freight from the Scales to the summit, but for a mere seven cents a pound, stampeders could have their outfits transported by CR&T's wagon and tram service all the way from Dyea to Lindeman City. Rather than continue to struggle against one another, the three companies soon merged and began advertising a new price of 10 cents a pound from Dyea to Bennett.

The old DKT boiler intrigues me for two reasons: its size and its location. I don't know whether it was dragged here in one piece or assembled on-site, but the thing is the size of a baby whale, and either way it must have taken a great deal of effort and money to get it the 13 kilometres upriver to Canyon City. To me that speaks volumes about the way people viewed the gold rush. It was a high-stakes

The Dyea–Klondike Transportation Co.'s power house at the summit drove the aerial tramway which supplemented backpacking for those who could afford it.

gamble, and each person who rolled the dice was convinced he or she was going to make a fortune. From the poorest Montreal seamstress to the wealthiest San Francisco investor, they took every penny they owned and placed it on the table. If they ended up breaking even, they could count themselves lucky.

After we've had our fill of marvelling at the boiler and speculating about how it functioned, we spend another quarter hour wandering around the network of footpaths that radiate from it. I spot a whipsaw blade, various cooking utensils and an abundance of flattened tin cans, some showing the lead seals that verify their age. A small flock of chickadees, kinglets and brown creepers also catches my attention with their high-pitched calls as they flit through the trees.

The only visible wooden structure is a collapsed cabin — a gold rush-era home that outlasted the rest because it was used for a while by hunters and hikers. How different it would have been to have come here in the 1950s, when there were still dozens of nearly intact buildings, and paintings could be seen hanging on saloon walls in Canyon City and Sheep Camp. With that much to see, we would have needed to add at least one more day to our itinerary. Already it's lunchtime

and we still have 7.5 kilometres to go. We return to the bridge and sit on the west bank, eating cheese and pumpernickel bread and the last of the cucumber, talking loudly to discourage any bears that might be considering sneaking up on us from behind. The turbulent river babbles back at us.

Back on the main trail, we soon find ourselves climbing once more. As the elevation increases, cottonwoods and spruce give way to western hemlocks, and the leafy understorey is largely replaced by a soft, thick carpet of moss. In places the steep grade and loose rocks make it hard to gain a foothold. The sound of rushing water fades away, and exertion causes us to suspend all conversation, leaving the silence of the forest to surround us.

About a kilometre past Canyon City the trail veers close to a precipitous drop-off straight down to the Taiya, 100 metres or so below. We walk cautiously over to the edge to peer into the gorge. Up the narrow valley, wisps of fog rise from the river, hovering like phantoms against the dark green, tree-clad hills before fading into the slate-coloured sky.

It was in a place like this that Lillian Oliver saw "a man, a raving maniac, whistling for imaginary dogs and calling partners, making the mountains echo and re-echo with his awful cry." When he spotted Lillian and her guide, he ran to the edge of the canyon, and she was convinced that if they had pursued him he would have thrown himself over the edge. She found some packers and told them about the man, thinking they would organize a rescue party to save him from his own insanity, but they brushed her off, saying there were many such men around and would be more before the season ended.

Although the hardships of the trail could drive a person to despair or even insanity in any season, this was a scene only a summer traveller could have witnessed, for in winter the stampeders kept to the bottom of the canyon — a deep, gloomy, three-kilometre-long trench. Pulling their loaded sleds over rough ice, slippery rocks and fallen trees was not easy, but it was faster than bypassing the canyon on the warm-weather trail. Stampeders who took the summer high road frequently complained about mud, boulders and numerous abrupt descents and ascents to cross streams and gullies that cut across the path. The modern hiking trail is still somewhat of a roller coaster, but a better-maintained one.

Up and down we go, stopping once or twice to fill our water bottles or eat handfuls of dried fruit and nuts, glancing at the sky whenever there is a gap in the trees and wondering if it will rain before we reach Sheep Camp. Except for one other group of hikers with whom we play leapfrog for a couple of kilometres, overtaking each other whenever we stop, we feel like we are alone out here. There are few birds moving in this forest, and the only ones I manage to positively identify are a family of young varied thrushes that fly up, with startled cries, from the ground where they have been feeding.

Here and there, we come across a downed utility pole with crossbars and metal fastenings, part of the Dyea-Klondike Transportation Company's electrical system. The last of these poles fell about a year ago and now they are all lying on the ground, slowly being obliterated by lichens and moss. The telephone line also ran along here, and the experts are still trying to sort out the origins of the different wire strands that appear at various points, draped along the ground and over bushes.

An hour or so after leaving the river at Canyon City we rejoin it at the point where the valley once again widens. Dubbed Pleasant Camp by the stampeders, this flat, open area was the first decent stopping place beyond the canyon. These days there are three Pleasant Camps: the Klondike-era site, which occupied both sides of the Taiya, with a bridge linking the two halves; the first official recreational campground, located about 500 metres beyond the main gold-rush site; and the new campground, another half a kilometre farther up the trail, which was developed after the river shifted course and began to run through the old campground in 1996.

During the gold rush, stampeders who had taken the high trail up and around the canyon crossed the river here, on a toll bridge that has long since been washed away. While they continued along the west bank to Sheep Camp, modern hikers stick to the east side of the river. With Sheep Camp and Canyon City so close, Pleasant Camp never developed into a proper town, but it did have a few amenities and was a popular midday resting place for travellers. As Sheep Camp became more crowded, stampeders were forced to pitch their tents farther and farther back down the trail toward Pleasant Camp, and by April 1898, the route between the two centres was solidly lined with canvas.

Both the old and new Pleasant Camp campgrounds are worthy of the name, though like the original, they don't get as much overnight use as other places along the trail. Today the clouds are hunched low over the valley, but I remember from my previous trip how refreshing it was to emerge from the sombre half-light of the dense coniferous forest to the openness of cottonwood groves scattered along the riverbank. That time, my companions and I lingered for a while beside the river, basking in the sun and admiring the rocky, snow-crowned peaks that rose all around us against a perfect cerulean sky. I have to admit, however, that my enjoyment of the view was tempered by the thought of getting over those mountains the next day. I suppose the silver lining to the clouds that are hanging over us now is that they conceal what lies ahead.

With no sunshine tempting us to prolong our stay at Pleasant Camp and the air getting noticeably cooler as the afternoon progresses, we push on toward our final destination. Although there is little elevation gain in the final three kilometres to Sheep Camp, I am more than happy to call it a day by the time we arrive at 3:45 p.m. My whole body is weary and my feet are sore, though not blistered. All I want to do is dump my pack and sit down, but it's not quite that simple. There are 25 tent sites to choose from, and only about half are occupied so far. Because of the bear hazard, we're not supposed to leave our packs unattended while we assess the relative merits of the available sites, which are strung out over a distance of nearly 200 metres. So Mark and I drag ourselves back and forth comparing proximity to outhouses, cooking shelters, bear poles and neighbours, and trying to fit our findings into an equation that will tell us which patch of ground to claim. We're both too tired to make a decision, and neither one of us wants to impose our choice on the other. Finally the approach of a large party of Germans who look far more decisive than us tips the balance, and we grab the site we've been discussing for the past five minutes.

The next hour passes in a flurry of activity: changing from boots to Teva sandals, adding layers of clothing, removing all edibles from our packs and sending them up the bear pole, pitching the tent, filling the stove, collecting water from the river, retrieving the food bag, boiling water, and then, at last, sitting down with a blessed cup of hot tea.

From tea we move on to aperitifs, in the form of a generous shot each of old-style Kentucky whiskey, then to dinner. On tonight's menu is quick-prep tandoori curry, my first freeze-dried meal in about 15 years. In the late 1970s,

A Camp Yarn

when I got my introduction to backpacking in the Rocky Mountains of southern Alberta, I was led to believe that freeze-dried meals in foil packets were essential for this kind of activity. Over the years, however, dehydrated and "instant" ingredients that could be used to concoct lightweight meals became more widely available. I refined my backcountry culinary efforts and happily left those foil packets behind. Carrying enough food for my usual three-to-five-day trips has never been a problem, but when I started making plans for this longer expedition, I decided it was time to revisit my past and purchase some ultralight provisions.

To my surprise the curry turns out to be spicy and delicious, a great improvement over the bland, mucilaginous slop I remember from my Rocky Mountain days and undoubtedly better than what the majority of stampeders ate. Lillian Oliver was one of the lucky ones. Her first night in Sheep Camp she enjoyed a substantial dinner of roast beef, steak and onions, macaroni, potatoes, pickles, pudding and coffee — the first decent meal she had eaten since she disembarked at Dyea and, in her estimation, a bargain at only 50 cents. She happily turned over the other half of that dollar to the owner of the Wisconsin House hotel for the unexpected privilege of sleeping on a feather bed instead of a hard bunk or the floor, which was the best one could hope for in most trail-side establishments.

In contrast to the solitude we experienced at Finnegan's Point, Sheep Camp is swarming with 50 or so people. Fortunately the rain is holding off, so there is no need for all of us to try to crowd into the two cooking shelters. Instead, most people gather around the single picnic table outside each tent. We see several familiar faces from the trail, including the young women from Canyon City, and many new ones. We also locate Adrian, whom we have not seen since we all left Skagway. Even in the city, Adrian's slight stature and straggly beard give him a somewhat gnomelike appearance. Seeing him out here in the woods, crouched beside an old stump that he is using as a kitchen table, I find the image even more fitting.

Mark and I set our stove on the ground nearby and trade stories with him about our adventures over the past two days. Then we get onto the subject of food. I am left speechless when Adrian tells us about the extra provisions he bought in Skagway before heading off. For some reason, all he could think of to buy was a bag of frozen mixed vegetables, most of which he subsequently jettisoned when, quite predictably, they melted and turned to mush.

During the ensuing lull in the conversation a boy comes over and asks if we've heard about the hikers who saw a mother black bear with two cubs on the trail today. They started singing opera, he tells us, until the bears ran away. Well, I think to myself, you never know how culture may serve you. He seems to want to chat, so I inquire about his age. He tells me he is 11 years old.

"Do you go out hiking a lot?" I ask.

"Actually," he says, "I'm surprised I'm doing this. It's only my third back-packing trip."

According to a study conducted by Parks Canada, the median age of Chilkoot hikers is 36 (two years younger than me). Looking around the camp-ground I can see that this statistic is based on a wide distribution, from children even younger than this boy to women and men more than old enough to be his grandparents. That evening, after Sheep Camp ranger Sarah Gorecki has told the assembled masses about bears, weather, trail conditions and Klondike history, I quiz her about the age range of people who have managed to successfully complete the trek. She says the oldest that she knows of was 94 and the youngest was four, not counting the babies who got a free ride all the way from their parents. Which reminds her about Gigi, the seven-year-old, 1.5-kilogram poodle who crossed the pass tucked in the front of her owner's jacket a few weeks ago — the second Chilkoot excursion for both dog and mistress. I fall asleep that night wondering what sort of story Jack London would have written about a miniature canine with a fancy French name.

Morning comes early at Sheep Camp, because by now everyone has heard that it can take 10 hours to cross the pass and get to Happy Camp. Around 5:00 a.m. I am woken by low voices and the sounds of people preparing to depart. I turn over and, with very little effort, slip back into slumber. The next time I look at the clock it's after 7:30. Time to get up, but there's no need to rush. Our summit day is not until tomorrow. Today, Mark and I are going on a tour of the original Sheep Camp with an archaeology crew. I've warned Adrian that this will be very much a rusty-bucket tour, so he's going to take advantage of being packless for the day and see what photos he can get on the first part of tomorrow's trail.

The ranger's residence is a little more than a kilometre north of the campground. With its tar-paper siding and vertical batting it resembles many of the buildings I've seen in archival photographs of Sheep Camp during the gold rush. Sarah, the effervescent ranger who presides over this end of the trail and goes bounding up to the summit almost every day, opens the door with a smile. She welcomes us into the warm cabin and introduces us to the National Park Service seasonal archaeologists: crew leader Eve Griffin and her assistants, Jun Kinoshita and Ken Graham.

Over coffee, Eve explains what they have been doing this summer and how this work fits into the larger picture. The place we are going to visit today was once Sheep Camp's western business district. During the winter of 1897-98, it is estimated that at least 20,000 people passed through Sheep Camp. The average stampeder stayed here two to three weeks, just long enough to get all his or her goods to the top of the pass. The more permanent population of entrepreneurs and employees probably numbered between 1,000 and 3,000. Altogether, the population of Sheep Camp on any given day during the height of the stampede was probably around 5,000 to 8,000 people, making this by far the largest community between Dyea and Bennett.

At its peak, Sheep Camp was a town of numerous hotels, restaurants and supply houses. Other businesses included saloons and dance halls, doctors and drug merchants, a hospital, laundries, bakeries, a meat market, a bath house, a lumber yard and a post office. Many of these enterprises were housed in hastily erected wooden structures, either log cabins or false-fronted frame buildings. On every side were thousands of tents, in some places packed so tightly together that it was impossible to walk between them.

Sheep Camp's commercial core extended nearly a kilometre along the river and occupied both west and east banks. The tents filled every other available space along the trail as far south as Pleasant Camp and some distance north toward the treeline, or what was the treeline until most of the forest was felled for cooking and heating fuel. Nearly all the businesses were clustered along the trail, which became the main street as it ran through the centre of town before crossing the river. Unfortunately for present-day archaeologists, in the years since the gold rush, the fickle Taiya has abandoned its 1898 channel and taken over part of the main street for its new course. At the same time, the rainforest has been doing its best to reclaim the ground it lost one hundred years ago. This is what Eve calls a dynamic landscape.

For the past three summers Eve has been involved in a systematic cultural-resources inventory of Klondike Gold Rush National Historical Park. It began at Dyea in 1984 and will end at the Canada-U.S. border a few years from now, provided funding is maintained. There is excitement in her voice as she describes the American half of the Chilkoot Trail as a "16-mile river of refuse," sadness and frustration as she laments the lack of resources to identify and protect all of this historical bounty. "The last standing tram tower collapsed in the spring of 1996," she says. "That's a good indication of the problems the park faces. It's impossible to preserve. At this point the priority is just to record."

Compounding the challenges of dealing with a dynamic landscape is the impact of the modern stampede of backpackers. While the majority resist the urge to carry away artifacts, even these law-abiding individuals may unwittingly do damage. Eve uses the example of a tram tower up near the summit that has fallen across the trail. "Everyone walks right over it," she says, sounding more resigned than critical. "They don't even realize it's there or understand what it is." Sometimes, however, the damage is more malicious. Until five years ago, the Sheep Camp campground was just north of the ranger's residence. It was moved to its present location primarily because it stood too close to the remains of a

Klondike-era warehouse, which was rapidly being destroyed by people chopping away pieces of its log walls to burn in their campfires.

Given what's gone on in the past, it is easy to understand why the National Park Service is not eager to advertise the exact location of West Sheep Camp. Fortunately, the task of protecting the area from souvenir hunters, vandals and careless sightseers is made easier by the fact that there is no easy way to reach it. The archaeologists get back and forth across the deep, fast-flowing river on a contraption known as a zip line. As I am about to find out, it's a bit like playing Spiderman.

Jun goes first, quickly stepping into his harness, snapping a carabiner onto the overhead cable strung between wooden scaffolds on either side of the river, and launching himself confidently out across the surging water. In less than a minute he has crossed the 60-metre gap and is standing on the opposite shore. Meanwhile, Ken is trying to get me into my harness, a complicated arrangement of straps and buckles that are supposed to encircle various parts of my body and hold me in an upright sitting position as I hang suspended from the cable. I'm not sure whether to be reassured or alarmed when he mentions that one particular fastening is to keep me from turning upsidedown. I make the mistake of asking why we have to wear climbing helmets for this aerial exercise. Coolly, Ken explains that if, despite all precautions, I do find myself making the crossing in an inverted position, the helmet is supposed to prevent my brains from getting bashed against the rocks. Good to know they've got all the bases covered.

Once I'm secured in my harness, Ken attaches me to the cable and instructs me to step backwards off the scaffold, pushing out with my feet. I do so awkwardly and swing wildly for a moment before remembering to reach up and grasp the guyline below the cable. Then it's a simple matter of hauling myself hand over hand to the other side. The ride is exhilarating and much too short. This has got to be one of the most fun parts of being a Chilkoot archaeologist.

The least fun part is removing one hundred years' growth of devil's club, alders and other assorted vegetation from the sites they wish to examine. The aptly named devil's club or Opopanax horridus is an especially fearsome adversary, standing one to three metres tall in dense thickets and armed with sharp spines all along its contorted stems and underneath its broad leaves — spines that readily break off and become embedded under the skin, where they fester for days or weeks. Eve is full of praise for the extensive brush-clearing work Jun and Ken have done during the past few months. The two men, who are both built like wrestlers, make little of their heroic efforts. They all know it's the only way to get to what really interests them. Some archaeologists dig in the hot desert; this crew slashes shrubs in the rainforest. Almost no excavation is required here because nearly all the gold-rush artifacts are lying on the surface or under a thin layer of leaf litter or river silt.

This is the second archaeological survey of West Sheep Camp. Much has changed since the first one was done in 1979. Eve leads us to a clearing and points out a square of barely discernible timbers that indicate where a building once stood. Then she pulls out a 1979 sketch of the same building, showing walls still standing to waist height, one of them holding an empty but intact window frame. "It's pretty disturbing what's been lost in the last 20 years," she says. "I think in five years there will be nothing left above ground."

All they can do is to carefully record the position of each identifiable building so those artifacts that are less prone to decay can be understood in context, even once all traces of the town's architecture have disappeared. A summer spent making careful measurements, plotting this information on maps and poring over archival photographs has given Eve an intimate knowledge of this spectral town. She leads us down the main street, pausing now and then to point out prominent businesses — the Mascot Saloon, the Seattle Hotel and Restaurant, T. Lubelski's General Merchandise retail store — as if they were still there, as solid and real as the day they were built. I can almost hear the clamour of voices, the barking dogs and the tinkling piano music coming from the dance hall just down the way.

The abundance of artifacts scattered everywhere we go makes me mourn for what has been lost in more accessible sites like Dyea and Canyon City. The most ubiquitous items, Eve says, are five-gallon kerosene cans, rubber boots, glass insulators, tin cans that once contained condensed milk and other foods, champagne and beer bottles, nails and sled runners. Also common is grey graniteware, the eating and cooking utensils made of enamelled iron that were an essential part of every stampeder's outfit. Each relic whispers a small story about this place and its inhabitants. At the Mascot Saloon, Eve pushes back the branches of an alder to show us the fanciful decorations on a woodstove. In its shiny, nickel-plated heyday, this was more than a heating unit. It was a symbol of opulence that promised the cold, exhausted men who gathered here that fortune awaited them at the end of their journey.

While I am drawn to items like the ornate woodstove, Eve sees the significance of more prosaic artifacts like tramway cables, or wire ropes, as she tells me they are more correctly called. "One of the most interesting things about the trail," she says, "is that it was so highly industrialized and attracted major investors." The high-tensile, steel-wire rope that the Chilkoot Railroad and Transport Company used for its aerial tramway was specially manufactured by the Trenton Iron Works in New Jersey. Because of the remoteness of the Taiya Valley, CR&T wanted cable that was as light as possible yet still strong enough to carry heavy loads. Their willingness to pay the cost of having it custom-made on the other side of the continent is an indication of their belief in the long-term viability and importance of the Chilkoot Trail.

At the end of our tour we return to one of the pharmacies, where Ken and Jun are down on their knees examining a collection of medicine bottles. The last time archaeologists were here, these bottles were neatly arranged as though they had been in a packing case that had rotted away. Twenty years later they lie jumbled on the ground and a few have been broken. The two men inspect them one by one, carefully recording the exact size, shape and colour of each bottle and noting any distinguishing marks. Reading the clues, they can tell where many of the bottles were manufactured and what they contained.

Once they have finished with this bottle cache, the archaeologists will have completed their work in West Sheep Camp. I had expected they would be collecting artifacts as they went, but Eve explains that this only happens in exceptional cases. Since the National Park Service is merely the manager of this primarily state-owned land (the city of Skagway and some private parties also have holdings along the trail), the cultural resources staff cannot remove anything without spending hours doing paperwork to obtain permission. Within a month or two, the buildings and objects they have worked so hard to uncover will be buried in snow. Next spring, new greenery will surge up and take possession of the town once more.

When we get back to the campground in the early afternoon we find it is already starting to fill. There is a rhythm to the traffic along this trail. It is as if each day the rising tide moves up the valley, gathering backpackers and carrying them to the foot of the pass. Then, in the early hours of morning, a rogue wave sweeps in and washes everyone in Sheep Camp up and over the mountains, dumping most of them at Happy Camp, while a few trickle down to lower elevations on the far side.

This movement is especially apparent now that the American and Canadian park authorities have started to limit the number of people using the trail. All backpackers must decide in advance where they will camp each night and exactly when they will go over the pass. Only 50 people a day are allowed to travel between Sheep Camp and Happy Camp. Each of us carries a backcountry permit indicating the date of our chosen summit day. My tag reads "17 Aug 98." Tomorrow, rain or shine, I climb the Golden Stairs.

Sheep Camp to Happy Camp

4:45 A.M. THERE IS ENOUGH LIGHT TO CHECK MY WATCH, BUT IN MY OPINION it's stretching a point to call this ungodly hour "morning." My alarm is set for 5:30. No chance of returning to sleep now, though. I lie in my warm cocoon and listen to the wind wailing in the treetops. Sarah's weather forecast yesterday called for a 70 percent chance of rain overnight and a 90 percent chance for today. So far we're still dry, but the odds of staying that way are not promising. I find my thermometer and put it outside the tent. When I retrieve it a few minutes later it reads 15 degrees Celsius, the same as it has every other time I've looked at it on this trip. I'm beginning to think the mercury is stuck. Anyway, I don't need a thermometer to tell me it's a cool day. I wriggle out of my sleeping bag and into several layers of warm clothes, including my beloved purple fleece pants, which I will wear until just before we're ready to leave. When I emerge from the tent and see a few patches of blue sky directly overhead, I enjoy a moment of optimism, which is squelched almost immediately by the sight of heavy, dark clouds to the north toward the pass. Better get packed and moving before the inevitable happens.

As at dinnertime yesterday, the two picnic tables outside the cooking shelters are the social centre of the camp. This morning, people who were strangers last night greet each other with smiles of recognition and friendly inquiries about how well they slept. Breakfasts are prepared and consumed with a degree of

Beyond Sheep Camp the trekker leaves the forest and enters the sub-alpine zone.

efficiency that reflects our shared desire to get under way. Conversation focuses on one thing: the critical 13 kilometres that we are all about to hike. Generally the tone is one of cheerful apprehension. One or two people seem genuinely

worried about their ability to make it over the pass. The veterans of the trail exude a sense of determined calm.

At 7:10 a.m. Adrian, Mark and I depart Sheep Camp. Although we have now consumed three days' worth of food, my pack is as heavy as when we began this trip. In order to reduce Adrian's burden and make it easier for him to capture today's arduous portion of the trail on film, Mark is carrying his tent, some of his stove fuel and his oatmeal supply.

The plucky women of the Klondike made their own contribution to the effort.

And because it doesn't seem fair to let my loyal companion take all the extra weight, I'm carrying a few items that normally would be in Mark's pack. Given that the tools of my trade are a simple notebook and pen, while a photographer's comprise many kilograms of camera bodies, lenses and film, I don't mind giving Adrian some assistance. This willingness to assist does not, however, prevent me from noting to myself that his load would have been more manageable if he'd invested in some lightweight gear to replace items like his heavy, rubberized rain jacket and overalls. On the other hand, Adrian may be harbouring his own silent criticisms of Mark and me for being walking advertisements for Mountain Equipment Co-op.

Personally, I'm happy to take full advantage of the improvements that have been made to outdoor clothing in the past hundred years. Oilskin coats, wool pants, leather mittens and hobnail boots were fine in their day, but I prefer the modern equivalents. I'm also relieved that the dress code for women has been relaxed. Back in the 1890s, propriety and fashion dictated that members of the weaker sex keep their bodies under wraps in corsets, petticoats, long sleeves, chin-high collars and floor-length skirts, even en route to the Klondike. The skirts were the worst. Typically made of four to nine metres of material, they were heavy and cumbersome, and their weight increased when they got soaked with rain. In winter they froze like hoops and in summer they dragged in the mud. Many women rebelled and raised their hems, only to be accused of being shockingly immodest for exposing their ankles. The bolder ones, inspired by the recent bicycle craze, wore long bloomers under skirts that came down only as far as their knees. The few that dared to appear publicly in men's trousers were treated as oddities at best and as brazen hussies at worst.

Before Martha Black set out for the Klondike, she purchased a corduroy velvet "outing costume" to wear on the trail. Decades after dragging herself over the Chilkoot Pass in this outfit, she still vividly recalled her chagrin when she realized how unsuitably dressed she was for the occasion. "As the day advanced the trail became steeper, the air warmer and footholds without support impossible," she wrote in her autobiography. "I shed my sealskin jacket. I cursed my hot, high buckram collar, my tight heavily boned corsets, my long corduroy skirt, my full bloomers which I had to hitch up with every step." The first time I hiked this trail it was a similarly hot summer day and I sweated my way to the summit in shorts and a T-shirt. Martha had my sympathy and admiration then and she has them now, even though this is not a day when overheating is likely to be a concern.

One kilometre up the trail, near the ranger's residence, we pass a low log building that used to be the shelter for the old campground and now houses an interpretive exhibit. Like the cabin at Canyon City, it was built by prison work crews in the 1960s. The rangers have placed a logbook in the cabin and asked people to comment on why they are hiking the Chilkoot Trail. Many of those who have recorded their answers over the summer say they came to enjoy some combination of history, challenge and scenery. For most people it is a once-in-a-lifetime experience, at least according to a 1995-96 visitor survey, which found that 87 percent of hikers on the trail were making their first Chilkoot

Pack horses worked long, cruel hours. Attrition among them was high.

trip. The logbook has quite a few mentions of people who are making the trek for the second, third or fourth time, so perhaps the gold-rush centennial has attracted more than the usual number of repeat visitors.

Flipping through the pages I also notice that a significant number of people have come to search for or celebrate family connections to the Klondike gold rush. A July 24th entry written by a woman from Bellevue, Washington, is typical of the mood and motivation of the descendants. "This is the 100th anniversary of my great-grandfather's stampede adventure. It's thrilling to be a part of this historical event and experience what he did." A 72-year-old Californian who stopped here the next day on her way over the pass offers a slightly different twist on the family theme. Her father had wanted to join the stampede when he was 19 but had stayed home to look after his mother instead. "So here I am," she declared, "doing it for us both." An entry from August 15 also catches my eye and makes me regret that I wasn't here two days earlier, when I might have met the pair who wrote simply, "A relived hike of the Centennial year when our ancestors (First Nations) guided the Europeans through their trading trail."

As we leave the cabin I become aware of a fine mist in the air. Knowing that we will soon be on our way uphill, I resist the urge to add another layer of clothing over my T-shirt. I am soon warmed by the effort of climbing, although the grade is still relatively easy. The increasing elevation is marked by gradual changes in the plant life. Many of the species I saw in the lower rainforest are still present, but the trees are becoming more stunted, leaving alder and willow shrubs as the dominant vegetation. Stately Indian hellebore, with its distinctive, accordion-pleated leaves, shows up for the first time along the trail, a sign that we have reached the subalpine.

During the gold rush, the five-kilometre ascent from the original Sheep Camp to the Scales became known as Long Hill. One stampeder who crossed the Chilkoot in 1898 described this section as "rough, rocky and bad smelling from the dead horses and dogs." It seems incredible to me that pack animals were forced to negotiate this terrain under full loads, but they did indeed carry freight, and occasionally riders, on their backs all the way to the base of the pass. In winter the horses' regular shoes were removed at the bottom of Long Hill and they were fitted with ice creepers to help them up the slippery slope. The inmates who worked on the trail in the 1960s found a pile of horseshoes as tall as a man's shoulder that marked the spot where the switch was made, but this collection has long since been reduced to nothing by the people who followed behind them.

Although it was the White Pass route that became notorious as the Dead Horse Trail, the Chilkoot also saw its share of the slaughter that was the great shame of the Klondike gold rush. Lillian Oliver wrote to her husband that she had seen dead horses all along the trail, lying where they had fallen and then been dispatched by a bullet or a blow to the head because they were too badly injured to save. The smell, she said, was "frightful." The sight that caused her the most anguish was the blatant mistreatment of animals by some of her fellow stampeders. "Nowhere on earth is man's selfishness displayed more than on the trail here. They lash and spur their poor horses up the mountains weighted down with heavy packs, and if they stop to take a drink they will get rocks thrown at them, accompanied by curses. Their tired dogs, also carrying perhaps a 50 lb. pack, they kick if one stops to rest. How my heart ached for these noble beasts."

Packhorses that escaped injury and death on the trail quickly became exhausted by the ordeal of working under these conditions. A few were hauled over the summit and used on the trail through to Bennett, but generally this was not considered worth the effort. Once stampeders got their outfits to the Scales, they sold their horses if they could find a buyer. Animals that were in such poor condition they could not even be given away were killed on the spot or left to die from a combination of starvation and exposure.

In September 1897, journalist Tappan Adney recorded his observations of the situation on the Chilkoot Trail, comparing it to the White Pass Trail (also known as the Skagway Trail), which he had investigated a few weeks earlier.

The cruelty to horses is past belief; yet it is nothing to the Skagway trail, we hear. There are three thousand horses on the Skagway trail — more to kill, that's about all the difference. Sheep Camp is filling up with broken-down brutes. Their owners have used them and abused them to this point, and are too tender-hearted (?) to put them out of their misery. Their backs are raw from wet and wrinkled blankets, their legs cut and bruised on the rocks, and they are as thin as snakes and starving to death.

Abandoned horses stumbled through town, causing havoc as they tripped over tent guylines and broke into food caches. Yet nobody wanted to take responsibility for killing them, in case someone suddenly came forward claiming to be an owner and demanding compensation. Adney was finally incited to action when "a wretched, thin, white cayuse" that had been driven down from the Scales and deserted at Sheep Camp sought refuge in his tent. "It was raining a cold rain," Adney wrote. "He put his head and as much more as he could inside the tent, trying to get next to the stove. He stayed there all night and was around all next day, and he had nothing to eat. I am certain he never felt the 44-caliber bullet back of his ear that evening. Thereupon a general killing-off began, until carcasses were lying on all sides."

Halfway up Long Hill we reach the beginning of the talus fields that dominate from here to the summit. From a geologist's perspective, this rubble, which has tumbled down from the surrounding mountains, is 160-million-to-130-million-year-old granodiorite — igneous rock classified somewhere between diorite and granite and composed of quartz, plagioclase and a little potassium feldspar (contributing a pinkish tinge), biotite and hornblende. From the perspective of most hikers, these rocks are simply an affliction to be endured.

Clambering up a large boulder in the middle of the path, I glance to the right and see a wooden grave marker among the lichen-encrusted rocks. It has been bleached white by a century of sun and snow, and the words that once identified the deceased have long since disappeared. This was the kind of end every stampeder feared: to die and be buried in some remote corner of the North with no kin at hand to tend your grave and keep your memory alive. Perhaps, however, the ghost of this hapless fortune seeker has found solace in being pitied incognito by the thousands who pass by here every summer.

This morning it is the desolation of this spot that strikes me. The sombre weather is no doubt an influence. I know from my previous trip that on a clear day, it is hard not to feel your spirits lifted by the scenic beauty of this part of the trail. As soon as you emerge from the tall trees of the rainforest, the mountains come into view, their lower slopes swathed in green, their rounded peaks frosted with ice and snow. Waterfalls glint in the sun as they tumble down to feed the Taiya River. Mountain goats are regularly sighted, balancing on impossibly narrow ledges or stepping daintily across the rocks. The Tlingits used to hunt these agile beasts in this area, using Sheep Camp as their base of operations, and there is some debate as to whether that site was erroneously named or whether there were also mountain sheep in the area at one time.

Adrian told me yesterday that he had seen a distant goat up this way while he was out scouting for pictures, but I am not expecting to see any today, since even the lower mountain slopes are hidden by clouds that are getting heavier and darker by the minute. The wind is also getting stronger. Around 9:30 a.m. we leave the last of the trees behind. From here to Happy Camp we will be fully exposed to the weather. A few minutes later I call for a rest stop in the lee of a boulder so I can put on a long-sleeved shirt against the bite of the wind and we

The end of the trail for some unfortunate soul.

Talus slopes above Sheep Camp herald the start of the summit pitch.

can both refuel. Mark and I are on our own now, having left Adrian farther
back, at his urging, so he can travel and photograph at his own pace. We quickly devour a couple of energy bars, even though I've mistakenly bought the brand
that tastes like Play-Doh, then drink some water to wash them down. The mist is
now bordering on drizzle. It seems not quite wet enough to warrant putting on
our rain gear, but we do decide to protect our packs with their waterproof covers. Before long, the mizzle starts to coalesce into distinct droplets and we pause
again to don our rain jackets. Other than these short breaks, we keep moving
steadily forward.

Where the trail is not rock, it's mud. But mostly it's rock. For long stretches there is no real path, just small cairns that indicate a route across a wide, grey
expanse of shattered granodiorite. Each step requires careful attention to ensure
the footing is firm, and while you're looking at your boots it is easy to miss a
cairn. Several times we have to stop and stare around for a moment before we
spot the next pile of rocks with its camouflage covering of lichens. The trail
alternates between hugging the east bank of the Taiya — here, in its adolescence,

a shallow but boisterous waterway — and traversing the talus fields. Several times the Taiya and its tributaries cut right across the route. Up here there are no such niceties as bridges. Streams are negotiated by eyeing the potential stepping stones in an attempt to choose the most trustworthy ones, then propelling yourself across in as few steps as possible. If you're lucky, you manage to keep your feet dry.

We pass a large iron wheel lying beside the trail, a reminder of the aerial tramways that ran night and day through the spring and summer of 1898, delivering nine tons of freight per hour to the summit. Unfortunately for the tramway owners, the completion of the railway line between Skagway and Bennett put an end to this profitable venture. In the spring of 1899, they surrendered to the inevitable and sold out to the White Pass and Yukon Route. WP&YR then took the precaution of disassembling the tramway systems and removing much of the equipment. The towers that supported the cables were left standing, but over the years they have collapsed one by one and their timbers now lie rotting on the ground.

There are flowers along the trail, too, but already most of them have bloomed and faded. I recall my first excursion over the pass, an early-August trip when the scree slopes closest to the streams were smothered with vibrant pink fireweed. This time I find myself focusing on lichens. They are not as eye-catching as the reindeer lichens we saw back near Canyon City, but they are the most abundant plants in this talus-dominated zone, because they alone have the ability to cling to bare rock and grow in the absence of soil. In fact, they are the soil makers, producing acids that dissolve mineral surfaces. Gradually, bits of crumbled rock and dead lichens accumulate in the cracks and crevices, providing a foothold for mosses and flowering plants. Lichens are ideally suited for unprotected situations like this. They can survive extreme desiccation by sun and wind, and their water-holding capacity is so great that they can increase their weight by 100 to 300 percent when moisture is available. The thing about lichens that really fascinates me, though, is that they are two species in one. As *Plants of Northern British Columbia* puts it: "A lichen is just a fungus that has discovered agriculture. Instead of invading or scavenging for a living like other fungi . . . the lichen fungus cultivates algae within itself." The algae's role in this relationship is to convert solar energy into food through photosynthesis. In exchange, the fungus protects the algae from the elements.

Lichens and rock, wind and rain. It seems as if the world has been reduced to these four elements. We have climbed right up into the belly of the clouds now, and the visibility keeps decreasing. The forested valley below us has been swallowed up. Now and then, the bases of the mountains are discernible, but there is no way of telling how high they tower above us. All that is certain is our own existence and that of the people immediately within our range of vision.

Our first two days out we rarely saw anyone else on the trail; today, other hikers are almost always in view. Normally I prefer solitude in the outdoors, yet it seems historically appropriate to have company when ascending the Chilkoot Pass. Besides, I'm gaining an appreciation of the kind of camaraderie that developed amongst the stampeders, one that also seems characteristic of modern travellers on this trail — a form of temporary friendship that can lead to shared meals and long, intimate conversations or might not even extend to an exchange of names.

The first time I hiked the trail, my party bore a strong resemblance to the kind of grouping that was so often seen during the gold rush. One of my companions, Suzanne, was the friend of a friend; we had talked on the telephone but never face-to-face until our prearranged rendezvous in Skagway. The other was a Norwegian woman, Guri, whom Suzanne met on the ferry to Alaska and invited to join us. We were strangers when we set off and friends by the time we reached our destination. During our trip we shared the campground each night with a group of Boy Scouts and became quite friendly with the two women who were leading them.

This time I haven't had the same opportunity to get to know my fellow hikers because no one else is taking as many days on the trail as we are, but I've noticed the same gregarious instincts at work. The Chilkoot throws together people who have nothing in common in their everyday lives and gives them a handful of perfect opening lines: Have you hiked the trail before? Are you ready for the Golden Stairs? Isn't the scenery wonderful? Isn't the weather terrible? Can you imagine what it was like during the gold rush?

Last night and this morning at Sheep Camp we ended up chatting with various members of an extended family as we cooked and ate. This is the third time over the Chilkoot for the oldest member of the party, a white-haired man who appears to be in his late sixties, the first time for his wife and the second for his brother. The couple's daughters, both in their mid-twenties, are novice back-packers who trained for months in preparation for this trip and have left husbands and young children back home in Juneau. The other two members of the party are the young women's cousins. One of these men is quiet and reserved; the other, who hails from Illinois, is an irrepressible comedian. I don't know any of their names, but I am enjoying sharing the trail with them. All the way up Long Hill, Mark and I have been trading places with the junior foursome. Each time we pass them or they overtake us, we trade encouragements and commiserations.

Long Hill is aptly named. Just when it seems as though it will go on forever, we come round a corner, slide down a ridge of rock and find ourselves in a flat-bottomed bowl. We have arrived at the Scales, approximately 530 metres above Sheep Camp and 840 metres above sea level. It was here that the professional packers stopped to reweigh their loads and calculate their fee for the final push

The aptly named River Beauty, a species of fireweed.

*Picking a path through the boulder field reminds us of the determination — the obsession — of those who, a century ago,
made dozens of such trips, hauling their ton of gear.*

to the summit. The unscrupulous ones often raised their rates at this point, leaving their clients little choice but to comply. This was the place of final reckoning, where the stampeders decided whether they had the money or the fortitude to transport their outfits to the other side. A lot of items that had seemed essential when they were leaving home suddenly became superfluous and were simply discarded.

As a result of all this unburdening, the Scales ended up with one of the greatest concentrations of visible artifacts anywhere on the trail, although it has been much looted over the years. In addition to the items that were left intentionally, there are those that were buried by snow and never retrieved. This was a major problem during winter, since a metre or more of snow could fall between the time a stampeder left one load at a staging point and returned with the next. Another component of the artifact collection at the Scales is the accumulated debris from the tramway offices, warehouses, saloons, hotels and restaurants that were all crowded into this small pocket of barely inhabitable ground. Being here in August, when nearly all the snow has melted on this south-facing slope, we get to see many objects that would have been concealed earlier in the hiking season.

Before the Klondike gold rush, most prospectors using the Chilkoot Trail were only going into the interior for the summer, so the outfits they hauled over the pass were fairly compact and manageable. Those who decided to winter over also travelled light because they could count on replenishing their supplies at one of the few small trading posts along the Yukon River. When tens of thousands of ill-prepared gold seekers started to converge on Dawson, however, the Canadian government became justifiably nervous about the prospect of famine in the Yukon Territory. Shortly after the North-West Mounted Police were installed at the Chilkoot summit in February 1898, Yukon Commissioner James Walsh issued an order that no one would be permitted to enter the territory without a year's worth of supplies. When NWMP Superintendent Sam Steele reiterated this order later in the year, he allowed that cash could be substituted for supplies to some extent. His version of the decree specified that anyone who was not a resident of the Yukon had to have "two months' assorted provisions and at least $500 in cash, or six months' assorted provisions and not less than $200 in cash, over and above the money required to pay expenses from the border to Dawson."

Six to 12 months' worth of food, plus all the equipment one needed to travel to the Klondike and get established, worked out to roughly a ton of goods. What that ton of goods should include was a matter of great debate for stampeders preparing for their journeys. Newspapers and hastily published guidebooks were full of advice. The Thomas Cook and Son travel agency ("Originators of the Tourist and Excursion System") published a typical list in the January 1898 special Klondike edition of *Cook's Excursionist and Tourist Advertiser*. It was based on providing one year's supplies for one man, and it indicated average prices charged for these items in major Pacific-coast outfitting cities such as San Francisco, Seattle, Vancouver and Victoria.

GROCERIES

300 pounds best flour $6.75
150 pounds best sugar-cured bacon 16.50
100 pounds small white beans 1.50
10 pounds oatmeal 0.25
20 pounds cornmeal 0.30
20 pounds best rice 1.00
25 pounds best white sugar 1.50
20 pounds good coffee in can 4.00
5 pounds tea in can 2.00
15 cans evaporated cream 1.50
10 pounds baking powder 4.50
2 pounds baking soda 0.15
10 pounds table salt 0.10
20 pounds evaporated potatoes 4.00
10 pounds evaporated onions 4.00
1 pound white pepper, ground 0.30
1 pound mustard 0.15
1 pint extract vinegar in can 0.65
20 pounds evaporated apples 1.50
20 pounds evaporated peaches 1.60

20 pounds evaporated prunes 1.00
10 pounds split peas 0.50
5 pounds dried raisins 0.40
5 pounds candles 0.45
Total $54.60

HARDWARE

1 Yukon camp stove, stovepipes and bake-pan $5.00
1 large steel frying pan 0.25
1 riveted coffee pot 0.50
2 miner's tin cups 0.10
1 bread pan 0.40
3 granite kettles — 4, 6, and 8 quarts 1.50
1 galvanized water bucket 0.25
2 granite plates 0.20
1 knife, fork, and 2 spoons 0.15
1 bread or butcher knife 0.25
1 can opener 0.05
1 double-bit axe with handle 1.25
1 hand axe 0.75
1 whetstone 0.10
1 hammer 0.50
1 auger and brace 0.50
1 jackplane 0.75
1 chisel, 1-inch framing 0.50
1 50-foot tape 0.50
5-foot whipsaw 4.00
1 handsaw, Disston brand, 26-inch 1.50
1 small try square 0.25
2 mill files, 2 taper files 0.40
1 folding draw-knife 1.50
20 pounds assorted nails — 4, 6, 8, 10, and 12-penny 0.75
1 special make Alaska steel pick and handle 2.00
1 drifting pick and handle 1.00
1 long handle miner's shovel (spring point) 0.75
1 short handle miner's shovel (spring point) 0.75
1 gold pan 0.40
200 feet 1-inch manila waterproof rope 1.50
5 pound oakum and calking chisel 1.00
10 pounds pitch 0.50
Total $29.80

CLOTHING

2 suits heavy knit underwear $6.00

6 pairs double foot wool socks 2.00

1 pair double foot wool German stockings, tufted foot 1.25

2 blue flannel overshirts 3.50

1 heavy woolen sweater 2.00

1 suit extra heavy Mackinaw coat and pants 7.00

1 pair each heavy woolen gloves and mittens 1.00

2 pairs wool-lined leather mittens 1.50

1 pair unlined leather work gloves 0.75

1 wind and waterproof duck coat, blanket lined 3.00

1 pair heavy duck pants, blanket lined 1.50

2 pairs heavy riveted overalls 1.00

2 pairs heavy overall jumpers 0.90

1 pair 8-pound blankets, any color 7.50

1 pair 6-pound all-wool blankets, gray 5.00

1 waterproof oilskin blanket 1.50

1 air-tight oilskin bag (for tea, sugar, etc.) 1.00

1 heavy duck tent, 8x10, Alaska style 8.00

1 pair heavy Giant Buckle suspenders 0.25

1 dozen best quality bandana handkerchiefs 1.00

1 heavy Scotch wool storm cap 0.50

1 stiff brim cowboy hat 2.00

1 pair high-cut 2-buckle rubber shoes 2.00

1 pair hip rubber boots (pat. duck kind) 4.50

1 pair specially made prospector's shoes 3.50

6 towels, toilet and laundry soap 1.00

6 dozen matches, pocket match box 0.75

Eye protectors 0.10

Buckskin gold bag 0.15

Rubber cement, rubber patching 0.40

Quartz glass, compass 0.90

Darning yarn, needles, linen thread, buttons, etc. 0.25

Pocket comb, mirror, toothbrush, etc. 0.25

Total $71.95

The profit motive spawned innovation in transport.

Cook's Excursionist and Tourist Advertiser did not mention specific requirements for women, but such lists were published in several other newspapers and guidebooks of the day. All emphasized practical clothing. One week after news of the Klondike gold rush reached the outside world, the *San Francisco Examiner* offered advice on what a woman "actually needs in the way of an outfit — presupposing, of course, that she goes the only way a woman should go, with a man who takes care of the necessary camping, housekeeping and food outfit." Among the garments on this list were gingham aprons and knee-length, flannel-lined wool dresses with matching bloomers. Moccasins and mukluks were suggested, in addition to rubber boots. A list that appeared in the Skagway News on December 31, 1897, included skirts made from denim, mackinaw (a heavy woolen cloth, usually plaid) or duck (durable, closely woven cotton or linen) and a hat with a brim wide enough to hold mosquito netting away from the face.

All through the winter of 1897-98, thousands of outfits like the one recommended by Cook's were transported in stages between Dyea and Bennett Lake. Stampeders who packed their own gear had to make up to 30 trips over the pass. Most men could manage only one or two trips a day, so their gear was stashed for weeks at a time, first at the base of the Golden Stairs, then again later at the summit. I look around the Scales area trying to imagine where they put everything. This is the first sizeable patch of level ground since Sheep Camp, and the snows of winter would have further smoothed out much of its unevenness, but it seems barely larger than a couple of football fields. Within this limited space there was, in the words of stampeder Alfred McMichael, who passed through in April 1898, "quite a village of tents, some bunk houses, saloons, restaurants, etc. and enough groceries and supplies to stock all the stores in Detroit." Although the crowds were small compared to those at Sheep Camp, the narrow alleys between the piled outfits were filled with people jostling one another in their hurry to move everything as quickly as possible so they could get past this barren, windswept spot.

When Mark and I arrive at the Scales, the only other party in sight is just departing. They quickly disappear into the fog, which has now reduced visibility to about 10 metres. We set down our packs and pull out gloves, hats and a bag of nuts and chocolate. It almost seems as if the thousands of voices that once clamoured here should still be echoing back from the cliffs. Yet the only thing I hear as I wander around examining the scattered artifacts is the sound of the wind. No running water, no birdsong, no shouts or whispers.

My reverie is broken by the voices of other hikers who materialize out of the fog. It's our friends from Juneau and Illinois. They pause for a quick look around without taking off their packs, then continue on. Time for us to get going, too. I'm sorry that we won't have the opportunity to stand at the base of the pass and view the famous ascent in all its intimidating glory. I remember how I stood here the last time, looking around and trying to determine where we were headed. Suddenly I realized the trail led straight to the vertical boulder field in front of us. It was as if some Neolithic giant's child had tired of playing with her stone blocks and dumped them in a huge pile. I had to get nearer, however, to fully appreciate the steepness of the slope and the size of the rocks. This time I'll only have the close-up view.

The footing turns bad immediately beyond the Scales. The rocks are furred with moss, making them much more slippery in the rain than the lichen-encrusted ones we have been walking on until now. The grade increases after several hundred metres and the moss disappears, but this is a mixed blessing. Now the real climbing begins and the illusions end. First to go is the romantic notion that this is going to be as effortless as mounting a flight of stairs, golden or otherwise. The name was a winter invention that came into use when a couple of enterprising men carved approximately 1,500 steps into the snow, strung a rope along one side, and charged a toll for their use. This being summer, we work our way up the 45-degree slope one boulder at a time. The smaller rocks, the ones the size of television sets, are frequently unstable. I test each one before trusting it with my full weight. The large ones, some of them as big as sports cars, are more reliable, but it is often a stretch to get a foot on top. Several times I resort to moving on all fours, pulling myself up on one knee, then rising shakily

Packing Up Chilkoot Pass

to my feet with my pack threatening to topple me backwards.

My fleece gloves are soon sodden from steadying myself with outstretched hands against rocks streaming with water. The rain lashes at our backs, plastering my hiking pants to my legs. Having left it too late to put on my rain pants, I've decided to tough it out to the summit and then change. My wool cap is so wet that it sags down over my eyebrows and water trickles down my face and neck. The wind grows stronger with every metre of elevation we gain.

Orange poles, thrust at intervals into the jumble of rocks, indicate a route that I can only assume is the best one. It all looks pretty much the same to me. Once in a while we veer over to the edge of the solid mass of mountain and scramble up a precipitous, muddy track for a while, then it's back out onto the boulders. My heart drums in my chest. I take in oxygen in large swigs, like a park-bench drunk who isn't sure the bottle will be passed his way again. My leg muscles start to protest against the constant strain of propelling my body and my load upwards against the force of gravity. Never mind, I sternly tell myself, just keep going. On a clear day, the spectacular view back down the valley encourages a more relaxed approach, but there's no joy in huddling in this deluge, peering into the fog. Our few pauses are brief. When we stop, I don't bother to remove my pack. It's easier to perch on a rock and let the weight of it rest on another one behind me.

An athletic Austrian couple whizzes past us, as agile and sure-footed as ibexes. Show-offs, I think uncharitably. A few minutes later we're the ones doing the passing, as we overtake another couple climbing at a painfully slow pace. Somehow they have lost track of the route and are out on the talus, while we are on the marginally better mud track to the left. Although they are only five or six metres away, there is no point calling out. The wind will simply tear my words to shreds. The woman seems half-paralyzed with fear, picking her way from rock to rock with uncertainty and trepidation. Perhaps she has already fallen. Her husband moves patiently beside her, one hand at her back, offering security. I look back a few minutes later and they are lost in the fog.

At the height of the stampede this slope was swarming with people. Tappan Adney described the spectacle in September 1897, as observed from below.

The men take up the packs. [They] walk to the base of the cliff [and] start to climb a narrow foot-trail that goes up, up, up. The rock and earth are gray. The packers and packs have disappeared. There is nothing but the gray wall of rock and earth. But stop! Look more closely. The eye catches movement. The mountain is alive. There is a continuous moving train; they are perceptible only by their movement, just as ants are. The moving train is zigzagging across the towering face of the precipice, up, up, into the sky, even at the very top. See! they are going against the sky! They are human beings, but never did men look so small.

The scene was altered in winter, when the climbers stood out in stark contrast against the snow and formed a continuous dark line all the way up the mountainside. Alfred McMichael, who went over the pass in April 1898, estimated there were 500 people on the Golden Stairs, their slow progress marked by a "steady tramp, tramp, up and up, here and there a place for three or four to sit or lean against the snow to rest, after which they again take their places in line." He had to wait 20 minutes for his turn to join the human chain.

Above all else, it is the winter photographs of the Golden Stairs that have come to symbolize the Klondike stampede. I studied these images before I tackled the pass the first time and foolishly thought it didn't look as bad as the written accounts suggested. My impressions would have been confirmed had the place where the antlike humans merge with the sky in the photos actually been the top. Unfortunately, as I discovered when I reached that place, it is a false summit. I gamely set my sights on the new horizon, but it too turned out to be a deception, so I resigned myself to climbing forever and was taken completely by surprise when we reached the apex of the trail. The total distance travelled is only 900 metres, but there is a 300-metre elevation gain over that short stretch.

This time I am prepared for the false summits. Also, it's easier not to get your hopes up when you can't see anything but the rocks directly in front of you.

Near the top, more evidence of 19th century mechanized ingenuity.

When we do finally reach that first slight levelling beyond which the stampeders in the photos all disappeared, I feel buoyed by the knowledge that we're halfway to the top. Onward. Upward. Time is blurred by the rain and wind. And then, without warning, the boulder field is funnelled into a notch in the rocks and the angle of incline decreases radically. We haven't hit the top yet, but I know the worst of the climb is over. The final section before the summit is through a narrow chute defined by rock walls that are higher than my head but not tall enough to shelter us from the gale. Instead they direct its full fury at our retreating backs, as though wind and mountain know this is their last chance to tyrannize us.

All the way up the Golden Stairs, lengths of wire rope that once supported tram buckets high overhead have paralleled our path, snaking along the rocks. At the top of the steepest section lies a gasoline engine believed to have powered a surface hoist, perhaps the one run by Archie Burns. We give it only a passing glance. My devotion to artifacts has been temporarily diminished by the weather, and what little enthusiasm I have left, I'm saving for a more intriguing spectacle I knows lies ahead — a collection of collapsible canvas boats that were abandoned near the summit during the gold rush. Not knowing they were there, I missed the boats on my first Chilkoot hike, and I'm determined to see them this time. Even so, when the marker that indicates where to turn off the trail emerges from the fog, I am tempted to ignore it. All I really want to do at this point is get to the warming hut that is just over the summit and change into dry clothes, but curiosity wins out. We turn and start scrambling up the rocks to the right.

The marker is a stone monument erected by the Alaska Purchase Centennial Commission in the summer of 1967. It bears a brass plaque that commemorates the Klondike stampeders, whose "tenacious spirit, dominating all obstacles, continues to inspire pioneers venturing north to the future." Apparently the government officials who were to hike up and dedicate the monument on August 6, 1967, were not sufficiently inspired to actually carry out this plan. The revised strategy called for them to be flown to Crater Lake in a floatplane, but poor weather nixed that arrangement, too. In the end they were flown to Bennett Lake and the dedication ceremony was held at the railway station.

The boats we have detoured to see — or, to be more accurate, the bundles of rotting canvas and milled lumber — lie a short distance beyond the marker, on a slightly higher ledge. If I didn't know what I was looking at, I'd be hard-pressed to identify these as unassembled knockdown boats. After all, even though I know the stampeders were heading to Bennett Lake and the Yukon River, this seems an unlikely place to find any sort of watercraft.

A deed of sale discovered in the Skagway magistrate's office by an archaeologist provided the first clue in solving the mystery of the boat bundles. It revealed that 232 collapsible canvas boats were shipped to Alaska, along with 49 sectional metal boats, by Flowers, Smith and Company, an American land development and transportation consortium active in the Lindeman Lake area in the winter

of 1897-98. It promoted its "nonpareil canvas compartment boats" as being convenient for transporting across the mountains and suitable for carrying a single man from the headwaters of the Yukon all the way to Dawson.

There are several theories about the company's abandonment of the boats. John Flowers's descendants believe that by the time the company got the boats to the top of the pass, the stampede was already winding down and there was no one left to sell them to. Others suggest that Flowers fell afoul of the Canadian authorities and his company was evicted from its base at Lindeman, or that the North-West Mounted Police prohibited the boats from being brought into Canada on the grounds that their poor construction might have endangered the lives of anyone using them. Whatever the truth of the matter, they are an interesting relic and worth taking the time to see.

Unfortunately, like many of the Chilkoot's treasures, they have been plundered over the years. When a member of the trail construction crew first came upon the bundles in the 1960s, there were approximately 200 of them. Only about 70 or 80 remain, and almost all of the missing ones are unaccounted for. Seven or eight of the bundles were removed in 1967 and distributed to various museums, and three more were later taken by the National Park Service, which dismantled two of them and used the parts to assemble a single boat. The restored boat, which incorporates some of the original cross-bracing, augmented with new wood and canvas, is 5.5 metres long, 1.5 metres wide and 58 centimetres high. A valuable addition to the material history of the gold rush, it has been displayed in Seattle, Skagway and Anchorage.

Once we return to the trail, the summit and the Canada-U.S. border — marked by a Parks Canada interpretive sign — are only about 200 metres farther on. By the time we get there we are too cold and wet to stop and savour the moment, but I feel triumphant nonetheless. We are standing 1,122 metres above sea level, and figuratively, if not literally, it's all downhill from here.

Hurrying to descend from these cold, blustery heights, I think sympathetically of the contingent of Canadian Mounties who had the misfortune of being posted here from February to July 1898. The role of the North-West Mounted Police during the gold rush was twofold: to safeguard the stampeders against the thieves and con men who circled like hyenas, preying on the weak, the innocent and the foolish; and to defend Canadian sovereignty during one of the most significant border disputes Canada and the United States have ever faced. It was the latter responsibility that demanded their presence right at the summit, rather than a more hospitable spot.

The problem was that the geographical boundaries of the panhandle region of Alaska had never been clearly defined, neither under the Russians nor under the Americans. Nobody worried unduly about this problem until the Klondike goldfields were discovered, suddenly demonstrating the enormous potential mineral wealth of the North and raising the question of which country was entitled to collect customs duties from the tens of thousands of fortune seekers headed for Dawson. The United States maintained that the territorial boundary was 16 to 19 kilometres inland from the Chilkoot and White Pass summits and therefore encompassed the entire length of the two trails. Canada's claim, on the other hand, extended almost to the mouth of the Lynn Canal and included Dyea, Skagway and Juneau. People like John Flowers, owner of the knockdown boats, were caught in the middle. As far as he was concerned, Lindeman Lake was in Alaska, so he proceeded to stake out a 32-block town on its shores and filed his plans for the new community with the U.S. government in January 1898. One month later, the Mounties arrived and sent him packing. This sort of confrontation fuelled the angry mutterings of nationalists from both countries.

In February 1898, Canada sent two 20-man detachments of Mounties to the summits of the Chilkoot and White Passes, where they each set up a camp, raised the Union Jack and began collecting customs duties. Both detachments were armed with rifles and Maxim machine guns. The Americans responded by sending 200 soldiers to Skagway and Dyea and demanding that the NWMP withdraw from the summits. When the Canadians refused, some American civilians began organizing to force the Mounties back to Bennett. Violent confrontation seemed imminent, especially since the American stampeders far outnumbered the stampeders of Canadian or British origin. People in the south spoke anxiously about the possibility of war. Fortunately, this tense situation did not last long enough for anyone to do anything rash. In March, discussions between the U.S. Army and the NWMP led to an agreement that the summits would be recognized as a temporary boundary. Two months later both national governments agreed to submit the dispute to arbitration. This had a calming effect on the situation, and the police detachments were able to move back from the White Pass to Log Cabin and from the Chilkoot Pass to Lindeman Lake.

The Mounties who were posted at the Chilkoot Pass probably remembered the months they spent living up there as some of the most miserable of their entire lives. The main camp was set up just north of the summit, at a slightly lower elevation, in order to gain some protection from the howling winds higher up. Pitching their tents on the flat surface of frozen Crater Lake seemed like a good idea, until a 10-day blizzard caused the lake to rise, spreading 15 centimetres of water across the ice. Unable to move camp in the middle of the storm, the men stoically hauled sleds into their tents and slept on top of them to escape the water. Meanwhile, two officers were toughing it out right at the summit, where they guarded the money collected as customs fees. Their tent was soon buried under three metres of snow. At first a guard was posted at night to clear the tent entrance every 15 minutes so the occupants would not be entombed within, but soon the snow won and they switched to sleeping in the tiny shack that had been built as a customs post. One of the men devoted much of his time to shovelling out the snow that unceasingly infiltrated the building, blown in between cracks in the planks. Firewood for the stove was often unobtainable. When it was available and the stove could be lit, the heat melted the frost on the inside of the building's canvas roof, resulting in an interior drizzle that soaked papers, gear and bedding.

Accommodations at the summit have improved tremendously since the gold rush. A small but snug patrol cabin and a day-use shelter for hikers were built by Parks Canada in 1989 and 1991, respectively, and it is with gratitude that I spot these two buildings a few hundred metres ahead as we start down the inland side of the pass. We are finally out of the fog, but for now, the stark beauty of Crater Lake and the alpine landscape stretching northward get no more than a passing glance. As we pass the patrol cabin on our way to the warming shelter I am puzzled to see three people huddled on the porch of the first building. I understand a moment later when I try the door of the shelter. Locked! Mark and I drop our packs and look at each other in dismay. The porch offers only minimal protection from the wind and rain, but we can't go on without changing out of our wet clothes. I start to dig into my pack and then pause, thinking how stupid it is to have a warming shelter that's locked on a day like this. I turn the door handle again, this time shoulder-checking the door with the full force of my frustration, and it swings open. Right then all I feel is relief. Later when we get to Happy Camp and find out that a party of Canadian soldiers had gone through ahead of us and failed to force their way inside, I feel slightly smug.

Mark yells to the people outside the patrol cabin and they quickly join us in the shelter. As they emerge from their rain gear I see that two of them, twins or at least closely spaced siblings, are only about 14 years old. The third still carries the softness of preadolescent puppy fat. One of the sisters asks with concern in her voice if we have seen their parents. We describe the couple we passed earlier on the Golden Stairs. "That was them," she says. "They told us to go on ahead and wait for them here." Thank goodness I got that door open, I think to myself, because it's probably going to be a long wait.

The two sisters seem to be holding up well, but their friend looks disheartened and cold. She is tearfully staring at her wet socks as though she isn't sure what to do, so I tell her to take them off and find some dry ones to put on. Meanwhile, Mark and I are stripping off our own wet clothing and changing. I'd like to make hot drinks for all of us, but I can't bring myself to unload half my pack to find the stove and the cooking pot. The girl with the socks has rallied and no longer appears to be in a prehypothermic state, so I'm less worried, especially since she and her friends have found something to eat. We pull out our own lunch of rye bread, pepperoni sausage and chocolate, and consume it enthusiastically while we chat with the girls about what living in Fairbanks is like. Not bad, they say, but the malls could be better.

By the time other hikers arrive we've finished lunch and I'm starting to get chilled from sitting still. More than five people in the cabin is a crowd, so we reorganize our packs on the porch and prepare to head out once again into the weather. The rain is still falling, but we have left the worst of the wind on the other side. It's 12:10 p.m. when we leave — exactly five hours since our departure from Sheep Camp. We've covered only half the distance we have to travel today, but the satisfaction of having the pass behind us is enormous. Going downhill seems too good to be true.

If there were more snow on the ground I'd be tempted to follow the example of stampeder Edna Bush, who had no patience for a ladylike descent. "I picked up a small piece of board," she wrote later, "and, using it as a sled, I tucked my feet up, held my skirts between my knees, and with one big 'whoopee' I was on my way." This late in the summer, however, the snowfields of the summit area have been reduced to patches, none of them more than a few hundred metres in length. The surface of the snow has been scalloped by the sun, creating an effect that reminds me of water being rippled by the breeze, though it is as solid as ice. A thin coating of hard-edged crystals the size of peppercorns makes it as slippery as ice, too. It would be easy to end up hurtling down to where snow and rocks meet abruptly, so I content myself with descending in a series of sliding steps, with one boot heel acting as a brake.

This pace allows me to admire my surroundings. Up here in the alpine zone, nothing grows more than a few centimetres above ground level. While hardy plants like mountain-heather and saxifrage can survive tucked in among the rocks, trees don't stand a chance. To some this might seem a desolate landscape, but after days in the rainforest and a morning wrapped in fog, I find the uninterrupted view refreshing. To the right, a mountain looms above us. Ahead and to the left, a wide expanse of open ground rolls into the distance, then rises to meet the clouds that hide the heights of Mount Van Wagenen. Crater Lake, in the foreground, is brilliant blue, despite the grey skies overhead. There is colour at my feet as well: watermelon-pink blotches on the surface of the snow, produced by a type of algae that specializes in living on this seemingly inhospitable substrate.

In between the snow patches, the trail is over loose scree. While it is no city sidewalk, it offers much easier footing than the boulders that dominated above the treeline on the other side of the pass. After a short, steep descent, we reach the flats along the edge of Crater Lake and the walking gets even easier. Hikers who make this trip earlier in the season, when there are still extensive snowfields in this area, have a more challenging time. Cycles of melting and freezing can make the snow icy and slick, and on sunny days the reflection can be dazzling. Before the invention of sunscreen and dark glasses, the local Natives used a mixture of soot and grease called kàtwat on their faces to reduce the glare and protect against sunburn. As the snowfields on the flats start to diminish in summer, a new impediment is revealed. Numerous small streams and meltwater channels intersect the trail, and the snow bridges that form over them can collapse without warning, plunging the unfortunate traveller into frigid, knee-deep water.

Once the snow clears, the streams are more of a nuisance than a danger. The volume of water fluctuates significantly, relative to the recent rainfall and the amount of snow melting higher up. Today, despite the rain, we are able to cross all but one stream by leaping from rock to rock. It takes us a while to decide on the best strategy for crossing the unjumpable one. Where the stream crosses the trail it is broad and relatively shallow, but there are no routes to the other side that aren't interrupted at some point by at least one wide stretch of ankle-deep water. It looks even less accommodating upstream, so we detour toward its mouth. After much discussion and walking back and forth, we finally decide that the only way we're going to keep our boots dry is to take them off and wade across at the narrowest point, even though this is also the deepest section. A small, midchannel island tempts us to try jumping, but the grassy banks are slick with rain, and I don't relish the thought of missing my landing by a few centimetres and ending up soaked to the knees.

Mark goes first and reaches the other side in moments. Feet bared, I hesitate briefly, then plunge in. The frigid water anesthetizes my tender soles against the discomfort of walking on the rocky streambed, and I'm across before I have time to get cold. While we are putting our boots back on, two members of the Juneau-Illinois party make their way down along the streambank to our point of departure. Wading is easy, we tell them, but they prefer a bolder approach. With a running start, they each make an impressive and successful vault to the island. The next stage, however, is the tricky one. The woman launches off immediately, using the momentum from her first jump, and lands with one foot on the bank and one in the water. Her boots are already so wet that it doesn't matter, she says.

A contingent of North-West Mounted Police kept the peace on the trail.

Her cousin takes a different approach, removing his pack and hurling it across the second channel. He follows it with an Olympic-quality broadjump, but his achievement is overshadowed by the fact that his pack, upon landing, has rolled right into a deep puddle. Fortunately, Mr. Illinois's sense of humour is still as vital as it was back at Sheep Camp.

After fording the stream we shift into forced-march mode. Ignoring thirst, exhaustion and aching shoulders, we push on relentlessly toward our destination, but I am not too tired to enjoy the sweeping vistas and the blue, jewel-like lakes and ponds. There are birds, too. A few gulls circling near a small island in the middle of Crater Lake. A female rock ptarmigan with a brood of young, their mottled brown plumage making them all but disappear into the vegetation. American pipits, identifiable by their dipping flight and the way they walk along the ground, bobbing their tails incessantly. In the dull light of this cloudy afternoon, the other small birds defy my attempts at identification. They may be snow buntings or rosy finches, both of which are often seen up here, or Lapland longspurs, which are less common.

Much as I appreciate the alpine landscape, I am overjoyed when I finally sight a grove of stunted subalpine fir trees. Happy Camp is at the edge of the timberline, so it can't be far now. I see a tent and then the roof of a building. We're here! It's 2:40 p.m. Total travel time: seven and a half hours. All I want is a hot meal and a cosy bed, but there is work to be done before I can have

Once over the pass, the lakes and mountains still to be traversed gave pause to weary travellers.

either. First we sort out the food and consign it to the bear-proof cache. Then, since Mark has Adrian's tent in his pack, he puts it up while I pitch ours, both of us struggling against the wind. Once I get our sleeping bags laid out inside the tent they look so inviting that I can't resist crawling inside and neither can Mark. Adrian arrives while we are napping and calls hello through the tent wall. We direct him to where his tent is awaiting him and he eagerly heads off to find it. It is still raining and hasn't stopped an hour later, when Mark starts nudging me toward dinner. I am loath to move, but at least I can look forward to a better meal than the kind offered by one of the few Happy Camp restaurants in 1898: a plate of tinned beef and a couple of slices of bread and butter, washed down with a cup of bad coffee. We have vegetable risotto with turkey on the menu tonight, and all we have to do to prepare it is pour some boiling water into the plastic bag that holds the ingredients, stir once and wait five minutes.

It turns out to be a good thing we saved our easiest meal for tonight. Not only am I exhausted, but the shelter is as crowded as the New York subway during rush hour. The cabin is only about three metres wide and 4.5 metres long, with a one-metre-deep porch off the front, but there are probably 25 people inside when we arrive to have dinner. Some are gathered around the table in the centre preparing food. Others sit on the benches along the walls, eating and just keeping out of the weather. Although there is no woodstove because of the lack of fuel up here in the subalpine, our cooking stoves and bodies throw off so much heat that we have to keep the four small windows cracked open. Sodden clothing crammed onto the numerous lines that have been strung across the room creates a steam-laundry atmosphere. Nobody seems to care that nothing is actually drying more than a token amount. We are all simply content not to be out on the trail getting wetter.

The camaraderie I had observed earlier is stronger than ever now that we have shared the experience of crossing the Chilkoot Pass in such abysmal conditions. This sense of fellowship makes me note with satisfaction the safe arrival of my Sheep Camp acquaintances. Mark and I had hiked the last half-hour with Carrie, one of the women from Juneau, who had pulled ahead of her sister and cousins. The last I had seen of the older members of that party was on Long Hill, where Carrie's mother already seemed to be struggling, so I am glad when she and the two senior men step into the cabin with tired smiles on their faces. The three teenaged girls and their parents show up around the same time, also cheerfully weary.

By the time we have finished eating our tasty and filling risotto, some of us are starting to feel concerned about another party that was with us back at Sheep Camp, a group composed of an Alaskan couple with their three children, aged six, eight and 10, and a mother with her 12-year-old son, from British Columbia. I had noticed when we were leaving that they were still airing their sleeping bags and seemed far from being ready to leave. The thought of them being alone on the trail at the end of the day is worrisome, but there is little we can do. When they finally walk through the cabin door at about 7:00 p.m., they receive an enthusiastic reception that probably takes them by surprise. The children are pale with fatigue, but the adults manage to summon enough energy to organize dry clothes and dinner almost immediately, and are admirably patient with their sluggish offspring.

At 8:00 p.m. I'm back in my sleeping bag trying to record some of the experiences of the day in my notebook. I manage to write only a few lines before sleep overtakes me. The wind has not quit blowing and the rain is still beating on the tent fly, but I don't care. As Lillian Oliver put it, "Here I am, safe and sound over the much-dreaded Pass."

Happy Camp to Lindeman City

IN THE MIDDLE OF THE NIGHT I AM AWAKENED BY THE NEED TO ANSWER THE CALL of nature. When I crawl out of the tent I discover that the rain has ceased and the sky has started to clear. Behind the tattered clouds, stars punch through the blackness. This is the first time I have been able to see them on this trip. I return to bed feeling at peace with the world and optimistic about our chances of drying all our wet clothes in the morning.

I'm also optimistic that Adrian will be able to compensate for yesterday's bad photographing weather by hiking back toward the pass without the burden of his big pack and getting some clear shots of the summit area. Knowing how unreliable the weather on the pass can be, I had advised him to book two nights at Happy Camp. I make a mental note to tell him about the collapsible boats in the morning so he can be sure to take some pictures of them. Then I drift back to sleep.

The next thing I know, someone is saying an urgent good morning right outside our tent. It's Adrian.

"Good morning," Mark answers.

I open my eyes and see sunshine illuminating the interior of the tent. "What time is it?" I ask.

"Seven-thirty," says Adrian, "and I'm leaving soon."

For one second I think he's heading off to capture some daybreak images

The azure waters next to the Deep Lake campground make a rest stop here a delightful one.

and I am about to comment on the dedication of photographers compared to lie-abed writers, until he adds, "I'm going all the way to Lindeman, so I need my stuff — the stove fuel and the food you were carrying."

"What about the pass?" I say. "It's going to be a perfect day."

"My sleeping bag is wet. I forgot to wrap it in plastic yesterday, until I got up to the summit. I hardly slept last night."

"But the photos?"

"I've got to get off the trail," he says emphatically. "It's a matter of survival."

"Hang on," Mark says. "I'll get up and find your things."

Remember all the trials gold rush-era photojournalist Tappan Adney faced when he joined the stampede on assignment for *Harper's Weekly* and the *London Chronicle*. Among other incidents, Adney had nearly all his photographic equipment destroyed by salt water when a storm-driven tide inundated the beach at Dyea. His outfit and many others had been carelessly left by a contractor who was supposed to have stowed the gear in a safe place after unloading it from the boats. By the time they found their goods, every bag of clothes and every box of equipment was wringing wet. Adney's cameras and lenses had come directly from the manufacturer in tins that were supposed to have been "hermetically sealed." As he opened each one, water poured out. His entire stock of cut film — 250 plates stored in pasteboard boxes — was also ruined. All that was spared was his 1-by-2-inch camera and a few rolls of film that he had been carrying separately. Thoroughly depressed, he sent a message south ordering replacement film that would, if he were lucky, reach him by parcel express in Dawson that winter. It was too late in the year for him to wait for a shipment to be sent to Dyea and still reach the Klondike before freeze-up.

As it turned out, however, Adney did not have to make his meagre supply of 1-by-2-inch film last all the way to Dawson. While he was at Sheep Camp, the owner of the hotel where he was staying asked him if he wished to buy three spools of film that had been left behind by a previous guest. Although it was four-by-five-inch film, he bought it without hesitating. By sheer coincidence, later the same day another man walked up to him and produced a four-by-five-inch camera and nine unused spools of film, which he also offered for sale. Adney leapt at the opportunity and with his revitalized photographic outfit, went on to capture many striking images of the stampede and the goldfields.

Three days after Adney and his companions rescued their gear from the waters of the Taiya Inlet, they were still drying out clothes and blankets. Here on the more arid side of the mountains we have a much easier time of it. In addition to the lines in the cabin and the ones strung across the porch, the bushes and rocks all around the site are festooned with gear. The breeze and the sun are already having an impact, although the air is still cool. I look at another camper's thermometer at about 9:30 a.m., just as the sun is appearing over the ridge, and it reads 10 degrees Celsius. Mine is stubbornly maintaining that it is 15 degrees Celsius, so I now know it is definitely not functioning.

A feeling of ease that permeates the camp this morning. Mark and I are feeling particularly relaxed because we have only four kilometres to hike to our next stopping place, Deep Lake. We have decided not to set off until all our things are dry, so I am sitting on the cabin steps drinking coffee, writing notes and watching a gang of arctic ground squirrels try to beg food from a man who is washing his dishes at a screened hole known as a grey-water pit.

We didn't see any grey-water pits on the first half of the trail, but apparently this is only because they have been temporarily removed from the campgrounds in order to install better ones. In the meantime, the authorities on the American side are asking campers to wash their dishes (with biodegradable soap) in the fast-flowing waters of the Taiya, which quickly whisks away any stray food scraps and removes odours that might attract bears. On the inland side, the campgrounds are beside lakes and low-volume streams. They lack the self-cleaning capacity of the Taiya, which discharges up to 710 cubic metres of water per second in summer. With grey-water pits, the idea is that campers will carry water from the lake or creek to the pit and, after washing their dishes, scrape any edible remains off the screen and carry them out as garbage. The pits are situated near cooking shelters to keep all food smells confined to one area. Unfortunately, many people don't bother using the pits, and those that do often neglect to clean the screens. The ground squirrels at Happy Camp are well aware that this is a good place to find tidbits like oats, rice and noodles.

Arctic ground squirrels are an interesting reminder of this region's glacial history. During the Pleistocene epoch, one of the few areas north of the 49th parallel that remained ice-free was the northern portion of Alaska and the Yukon, a region referred to by geographers as Beringia. Centuries of living in isolation from their southern relatives caused many Beringian plants and animals to evolve into separate species by the time the ice sheets melted away 10,000 years ago. The arctic ground squirrel is a good example of this process of division and speciation. Out of necessity, these rodents became specialists in coping with northern conditions like permafrost and a short breeding and feeding season. As the glaciers retreated they moved south, but not too far beyond familiar ecosystems. This northwest corner of British Columbia is one of the most southerly places in which this species is found.

My attention shifts randomly between the ground squirrels, my notebook and the panorama before me. Round-shouldered mountains rise in every direction, their lower slopes cut with green, their heights daubed with white. Down the hill from the cabin, Coltsfoot Creek sparkles in the sun. This shallow watercourse is one of the countless tributaries that feed the fifth-longest river in North America, the Yukon, which measures more than 3,000 kilometres from its headwaters to its mouth and encompasses more than 800,000 square kilometres of land within its drainage basin.

A wildflower welcome awaits hikers in the high country.

All the way down from Crater Lake, Coltsfoot Creek has been splitting and merging and weaving its way over the glacial till that covers the base of this high valley. At Happy Camp it is still wide and capricious, but just beyond this point it will be constrained by the precipitous walls of Coltsfoot Canyon. On this side of the creek, the slope down to the water is only moderately steep, but across from the campground, a steep cliff marks the beginning of the canyon.

I am just getting down to some serious writing when I hear people exclaiming and look up to see them pointing at a caribou standing on top of the high bluff on the opposite side of the creek. This majestic animal returns our stares with a steady gaze, then lowers his head to graze. While others scramble for cameras, I run back to the tent for our binoculars. After Mark and I each take a quick look through the binoculars, we pass them around. The caribou doesn't move. The binoculars make another circuit, with everyone taking as much time as they want to focus on the plushiness of his dark brown coat and the graceful sweep of his multipronged antlers.

Caribou are unique among members of the deer family in that both males and females grow antlers. Mature bulls, like this one, bear larger racks than females or young males. They can also be distinguished by the presence on one or both antlers of a brow tine that points forward and down off the main beam, apparently acting as an eye shield during combat.

After a while the caribou lies down and his admirers begin to disperse. I return to my writing but glance up every now and then to see if he is still there. He stays at his post for about an hour, then disappears as unobtrusively as he arrived. I assume that he is part of the Carcross-Squanga woodland caribou herd. The 450 members of this subpopulation spend their summers in alpine areas and their winters in mature coniferous forests. Much of the herd's range is in the Yukon, but in summer their travels take them as far into British Columbia as the southern ends of Tagish and Atlin Lakes. The town of Carcross — an abbreviation of "caribou crossing" — was so named because these animals once congregated there twice a year to ford the shallow waters at this junction between Bennett and Tagish Lakes. Since the early 1900s, no caribou have been seen at the crossing. Overhunting and habitat disturbance have taken a toll on the Carcross-Squanga herd, as they have on other herds in this region, and they are all now under the watchful eye of a government recovery program.

By late morning all but one other couple have left Happy Camp. Many of the people who camped here last night will see each other again later today, but we have said our final good-byes to our summit companions. At last we begin our own preparations for departure. The tent and all our clothes are dry, so packing is easy. After lunch, we finally hit the trail at 1:30 p.m.

I am grateful to have a lighter pack today and only a short distance to go. My body is still weary from yesterday's ordeal. Deep Lake is at a slightly lower elevation than Happy Camp, but Coltsfoot Canyon forces the trail to take a detour over an area of higher ground between the two sites. A short distance beyond the campground, the trail turns away from the creek and climbs about 100 metres to a shelf that parallels the water. When we reach the top, we pause and look back. Earlier there was a sprinkle of new snow on the mountains back near the pass. Now the heat of the sun has set the slopes streaming with water, making the mountains look silver plated.

Being up above the timberline, amongst all this naked rock, gets me thinking about mountains as mountains. It is like seeing the skeleton of an animal and being reminded that this framework gives the animal its form, instead of being distracted by fur or feathers or the size of the ears. These particular mountains are part of the Coast Range Metamorphic Plutonic Complex (or simply the Coast Plutonic Complex), which begins near Kluane Lake in the southern Yukon and runs south for approximately 3,000 kilometres, cutting through southeastern Alaska and terminating near Vancouver, British Columbia. It is one of the largest masses of granitic rock in the world.

The Coast Plutonic Complex was first formed when an immigrant island chain known to geologists as the Insular Superterrane collided with what was then the western edge of the continent. Masses of molten rock flowed up from beneath the collision zone and crystallized. This slow-motion process ended about 45 million years ago. For the next 40 million years, the forces of erosion worked on the original Coast Mountains, reducing them to a mere shadow of their former glory, although their core still extended deep underground. Then, tectonic activity deep beneath the earth's surface forced a mass of fiery magma into position directly beneath the vestiges of this mountain range. As the thick crust of granitic rock was heated by the magma, it expanded and a process of uplift was initiated. Five million years later, the Coast Mountains, on which we are now standing, have risen some two kilometres and are still rising.

While fire gave birth to the Coast Mountains, it was ice that played the central role in shaping their character. The great age of glaciation, the Pleistocene epoch, began about two million years ago and ended about 10,000 years ago. During that time, climatic variation resulted in numerous glacial advances and retreats. By the end of the Pleistocene, the once-rounded mountains and the V-shaped valleys between them had been carved into new forms, and huge quantities of rocky debris had been gathered and redistributed. The highest mountains were sculpted into configurations that featured hanging valleys, knife-edged ridges called arêtes and angular peaks like the ones that define the distant horizon all along the Chilkoot Trail — when they aren't covered in clouds. Where the glaciers smothered the land completely, debris carried by the ice scratched and scoured the bedrock. Glacial striations, which are easily visible on the bare mountainsides between Happy Camp and Deep Lake, indicate the direction in which the ice flowed. Although the Pleistocene ice age is long past, a few remnant glaciers remain at high elevations and latitudes. Hundreds of these enhance the scenery along the trail, though only a few, like the Irene Glacier, are large enough to have been given names.

Beyond our viewpoint, the trail meanders across the side of the mountain. We pass several tarns — enchanting pools of clear water held in hollows that were scooped out by the glaciers — and a small bog with a flurry of cotton-grass blowing against the green sedges. Mountain-heather and crowberry have established themselves anywhere they can gain a toehold among the rocks. The only trees are those that exist as *krummholz* — a German word meaning "crooked wood." These stunted, contorted plants are shaped by repeated exposure to harsh winter conditions. Branches low enough to be protected by a thick blanket of snow can survive from year to year; the rest are desiccated by the wind and die away.

Below us, to the left, are the aquamarine waters of Long Lake, a classic finger lake, formed when an ancient glacier gouged a long trench in the bedrock and dammed the lower end with debris. Like Crater Lake and others we will see further down the trail, Long Lake owes its exquisite colouring to the presence of

First glimpse of Long Lake.

fine glacial sediments, known as rock flour, held in suspension. These particles reflect the green portion of the light spectrum, giving glacial lakes their characteristic colour. During the winter, most of the sediments settle, so in spring the lakes are at their bluest. As summer progresses and the alpine glaciers begin to melt, they deliver new supplies of rock flour to the lakes, which then become more emerald toned.

Because the majority of the stampeders travelled the Chilkoot Trail when the lakes were still frozen, they never had the opportunity to admire their colours. They did, however, appreciate the smooth, level surfaces provided by the ice. When the wind was blowing from the south, as it frequently was, they loaded their sleds with hundreds of kilograms of goods, rigged up sails and skimmed almost effortlessly over the snow. Those who had dog teams could also make fast progress. Even pulling a sled by hand across the lakes was easy compared to climbing the Golden Stairs, an ordeal that would have been fresh in everyone's memory.

In summer the lakes also played an important role in the transportation of supplies. Although Crater Lake was only three kilometres long, many people were willing to pay to have their outfits moved by boat from one end of it to the other, where they were then transferred to wagons and hauled to Long Lake. Another set of commercial boat operators plied this two-kilometre stretch of

water, landing at quays that are still visible near the Deep Lake campground. After being unloaded at the north end of Long Lake, the freight was either portaged around a brief but turbulent set of rapids and then ferried to the far end of one-kilometre-long Deep Lake, or loaded onto wagons and sent directly to Lindeman Lake.

Less than an hour and a half after leaving Happy Camp, we cross the wooden bridge that spans the short stretch of river between Long and Deep Lakes. Just past the bridge we climb up a few steps to the left of the trail and enter Deep Lake campground. During the past half-hour we have descended from the krummholz zone of the subalpine to the true treeline. The open forest here is very different from the dense coastal rainforest we left behind at Sheep Camp. The trees — at this elevation mainly subalpine fir and white spruce — are smaller than on the other side of the pass, and the understorey is not as lush. Instead of impenetrable stands of tropical-looking devil's club, there are loose blueberry thickets. This is one face of the boreal forest, a vast ecosystem that dominates the North from one side of the continent to the other. The coastal rainforest is shaped by the influences of a maritime climate characterized by high levels of precipitation and relatively moderate year-round temperatures. The boreal forest, lying in the rainshadow of the mountains, is much drier. The annual precipitation on this side of the summit ranges from 380 to 760 millimetres, about one-third the amount that falls at Dyea. Summertime temperatures are higher in the interior than on the coast, but in winter it is considerably colder.

Although Happy Camp was the first place north of the summit where stampeders could find any amenities, the encampment at Deep Lake was larger because of its more sheltered location and the greater availability of wood for fuel and construction. More than 100 tents and cabins were clustered near the boat-landing area. No buildings remain, but a number of artifacts have been gathered together up near the outhouse, and others lie half-hidden in the bushes. The modern campground is on the hillside looking east over Deep Lake. Instead of a cooking shelter it has a spacious eating area with two large picnic tables near the bear pole. Higher up the slope, about a dozen well-constructed tent pads are scattered among the trees.

We have our choice of spots since we are the only ones here, so we pick the one with the best vantage. We briskly deal with the essential chores of hanging the food bag, putting up the tent and organizing our gear. Then we each find a place to sit on the smooth, sun-warmed rock that surrounds our tent site and settle down to a blissful hour of reading, with frequent breaks to gaze about at the scenery. The air is redolent with the scent of the subalpine fir's aromatic needles. The swash and slap of the river surging over its stony bed below us is like a song in a foreign tongue. A golden eagle rides the thermals across the valley. I feel as if I could stay right here forever. Except that eventually the sun slides behind the clouds building to the south and Mark mentions dinner, which

Distant mountains signal that Lindeman Lake is still a hike away.

reminds me that, despite my periodic forays to collect handfuls of blueberries, I am hungry.

We have almost finished dinner when a figure appears on the trail from Happy Camp. A few minutes later he arrives, apologizing for disturbing our privacy and saying two more are also on their way to the campground. We assure him that we don't mind sharing the space. He's sensitive about overcrowding because of his experience last night at Sheep Camp, where a party of 12 commandeered one of the cooking shelters, leaving everyone else to squeeze into the other. He and his friends were supposed to stay at Happy Camp tonight, but they didn't relish the thought of competing with this group again. He looks exhausted, as might be expected, but says they had perfect weather for the pass — clear and sunny. I feel a twinge of envy, but today has been so delightful that the rain and cold that chilled me to the bone yesterday seem remote and not worth regretting.

The three new arrivals are eating dinner when we go to bed. By the time we get up in the morning, they have departed and we are once again alone. Because most hikers pass by the campground without stopping, the blueberry bushes are loaded. While Mark makes coffee I go foraging, quickly collecting enough plump berries to completely smother our oatmeal.

It is not as sunny this morning as it was yesterday, but it is sufficiently warm that we decide a little bathing is in order. First we haul water from the river and take turns helping each other wash our hair over the grey-water pit. It numbs the brain but ultimately feels terrific. Then we heat some water and take advantage of our solitude to bare our bodies and wash away the sweat and grime of the past five days. Using our cooking pot for a basin reminds me of Martha Black's eye-opening experience near the beginning of her trip to the Klondike with her brother George in 1898. One morning after she had finished doing the breakfast dishes, he asked her for the dishpan so he could wash his socks. When she objected strenuously, George answered, "Well, you needn't get so huffy about it. I took a bath in it last night." And with that, this well-bred Victorian lady resigned herself to the fact that life on the trail was not going to be the same as it had been back in Chicago.

I am just buttoning up my shirt when the first of the people who spent last night at Happy Camp show up. It's about 10:30 a.m., which means they probably started hiking when we were still in bed. It's enough to make one feel slothful, but I am becoming convinced that this trail is best taken slowly, with plenty of time for relaxation and contemplation. On my first Chilkoot trip, Deep Lake was just part of the scenery unrolling before me, too quickly left behind. Overnighting here this time has given me the opportunity to look more closely at the mountains and experience the high country with all my senses. Only now am I ready to move on.

Today's hike to Lindeman Lake is just under five kilometres long and down-hill all the way. It begins by skirting the marshy shore of Deep Lake, which is mirror-smooth this morning. At the north end, a collection of artifacts — including sled runners and a small horseshoe, no bigger than my hand — provide a glimpse of the many forms of transportation that were used along this route. Most prominent is the remains of a collapsible boat resting on a mat of crowberry, as if it had been pulled from the lake and left for someone who never came to claim it. The rusty iron frame was undoubtedly carried over the pass in pieces, then bolted together to form a vessel about five metres long and one metre wide. Only a few small fragments of canvas still cling to the ribs. Was it abandoned because it had already proved worthless on the water, or did it earn someone good money carrying freight on Deep Lake until the day when there were no more stampeders coming over the Chilkoot?

Just past these artifacts, Deep Lake pours into Moose Creek, which is almost immediately funnelled into Deep Lake Gorge. Within a few minutes the trail brings us to a viewpoint on the rocky terrace to the west of the gorge, where we can look down at the tumbling water constrained between the sheer walls. In summer, rapids and waterfalls made the river between here and Lindeman Lake impassable for boats. In winter, stampeders pulled their sleds over its frozen surface. The advantage, presumably, was that there were no trees or bushes to impede them, but descriptions of this section of the trail indicate that going downhill could be almost as difficult as going up had been.

Alfred McMichael found Moose Creek one of the more challenging stretches during the series of trips he made to haul his gear down from the summit in April 1898. After Deep Lake, he wrote in a letter home,

We passed through two canyons. These are very steep. [The stream] goes in leaps and bounds with falls from 2 to 20 feet. The sides are almost perpendicular and in many places the snow must be from 50 to 100 feet deep where it has drifted in. The trail goes right over this stream and is very rough . . . . Some places are very steep and it is almost like jumping over a small cliff with a sled loaded and one shoots down very quickly. Sometimes the sled tips over or gets stuck and that keeps everybody back, for most places there is only room for one in the narrow path cut into the big drifts . . . . The longest canyon is a bad place to get through and the trail is so crowded that often the men have to wait for hours to get through . . . . Once I had to wait 2 hours in a blinding snow storm.

Although Moose Creek descends from Deep Lake in a series of precipitous steps, the trail is gradual and easy. As we lose elevation, subalpine fir and white spruce give way to lodgepole pine, underlain by a jade-green carpet of creeping kinnikinnick studded with red berries. The river is now far below us at the bottom of a deep canyon with crumbling, buff-coloured walls. We follow its course for a while. Then the trail pulls away from the edge of the canyon and slips into the forest. The freight wagons and stampeders who came through when Moose Creek was not frozen took a more direct route from Deep Lake, following the ridge instead of the river.

Our next view of water is our first glimpse of Lindeman Lake, which soon emerges in all its splendour as we come down the hill toward the site of gold rush-era Lindeman City and the modern campground. The first thing I notice is the colour of the lake — an opalescent blue that is not as clear as, but no less lovely than the crystalline waters of the alpine and subalpine lakes. The Tlingits called this body of water Tl'ûxh'u Â, which translates as "murky lake," a far more meaningful identifier than the one that has been on the maps ever since Lieutenant Frederick Schwatka passed through here in 1883. The Lindeman for whom Schwatka named this lake was a German botanist and the secretary of the Bremen Geographical Society, which had sponsored a German expedition to the area two years earlier. It is doubtful he ever laid eyes on his namesake, with its milky waters and its backdrop of green hills and snow-capped mountains.

In the words of Tappan Adney, "The drop of eight hundred feet in elevation from Long Lake to Lindeman puts one in a new and smiling country." Lindeman City was built on a large, flat triangle of land that projects out into the lake near the south end. Originally this peninsula was forested, like the rest

of Lindeman's shores. By the time Adney arrived in late September 1897, much of the surrounding area had already been cleared of timber, most of it to be used for boat-building. The nearest trees suitable for this purpose, he reported, were now three kilometres back up the trail or across the lake and eight kilometres up its main tributary. Even these trees were of poor quality for sawing into boards. Adney was pleased to have had the foresight to bring his own lumber with him all the way from Victoria, although the cost of having it packed over the pass had been inordinate.

Adney counted 120 tents at Lindeman and 60 boats in the process of being built. The pace of work was frenzied, with everyone rushing to get on the water while there was still a chance of reaching Dawson before the onset of winter. Boats were being launched at the rate of six to 10 a day, but not everyone was able to leave before freeze-up. Adney, who set sail on October 6, was one of the last to leave. When winter began in earnest, Lindeman City, as the community was coming to be known, had about 1,000 inhabitants. By springtime, the number had quadrupled and businesses such as hotels and bakeries had been established. There were few wooden buildings, but to say that this was a city of tents gives little idea of the refined lives that some stampeders managed to lead under canvas, especially when they had to remain in one place for some time.

The Craig party — Mr. and Mrs. Morte H. Craig, their nine-year-old daughter Emily and Morte's sister Lulu, a teacher on leave from her school in Missouri — were among those who refused to let their situation lower their standards. In Lulu's memoir of their Klondike experience she wrote that they "enjoyed the novelty of camp life" at Lindeman City from March to June of 1898. Because the Craigs were planning to set up house in Dawson, they had with them china, silver, tablecloths, napkins and doilies that they unpacked and used here. Their provisions included not only the usual beans, bacon and flour, but also such luxuries as tinned oysters, lemons, figs, nuts, cheese and maple sugar. Their large tent had bedrooms partitioned off, and they slept in down sleeping bags on pine-bough mattresses that were replaced whenever they started to flatten out. The main living area was furnished with a table and stools, a settee, a bookcase and a china press, all built on-site. While Morte supervised the construction of their boat, the women "led a very busy life with [their] domestic duties and reading, writing, walking and chatting with friends."

Lindeman's last residents departed in the fall of 1899, and nature immediately began reclaiming its own. The plants that ecologists call pioneers — lodgepole pine, trembling aspen, fireweed and others — quickly recolonized the cleared land, just as they would in the aftermath of a forest fire. The numerous stumps still visible among the pines represent a white-spruce climax forest that will probably take another 200 years to become reestablished.

Lindeman campground is more spread out than any of the others along the trail. So much so, in fact, that signposts are necessary to help hikers find their

Beyond Deep Lake the trail skirts a rugged canyon.

way around. At the base of the hill we reach the main intersection and decide to check out the south camping area first. Part of its appeal is that it is near a swampy corner of the lake where moose are often seen grazing. I also have fond memories of staying here on my last trip, when I woke early in the morning and walked along the narrow, sandy beach to the tip of the peninsula. As I sat there by the glassy lake, looking at the snow-etched mountains, a gull came gliding over the water like a fragment of some glacier that had been released into the sky. It broke the silence with a mournful cry, then swooped down and landed gently amidst the reflected peaks. That breathtaking moment makes me want to camp here again, but this is not to be. A group of 12 mostly middle-aged men and women wearing red T-shirts that identify them as "Wally's Ramblers" has already claimed most of the sites.

Five minutes of walking takes us across the peninsula to the north camping area, as yet virtually unoccupied. A quick reconnaissance indicates that it is the superior site anyway. It is more sheltered from the stiff breeze blowing from the south and has a much better water source, since this is where Moose Creek enters the lake. At each of the camping areas there is a log cabin with tables and benches inside and a picnic table outside. Only the cabin in the south camping area has a woodstove, but this is not a concern for us, since the weather is fine. The cabins were built by work crews from the Yukon Correctional Institute in 1968 and 1970, and provided housing for the men during the five summers they spent clearing the Canadian portion of the trail and building bridges. These days, Parks Canada maintenance workers and wardens live in a seasonal encampment on the north side of the peninsula. Near the warden station there is also a tent that houses an interpretive photo exhibit and a small library. The fact that this is only a few hundred metres from our campground is a great attraction for a person like me who can't resist a collection of books.

Mark and I spend the rest of the afternoon reading peacefully in the warm sunshine. After dinner and cleanup, we walk back toward the south camping area and climb up to the Lindeman cemetery, reaching the top of the stairs just as the sun drops behind Mount Harvey. Although the view from here is magnificent, the place has a forlorn air. I count 11 rocky hummocks, each enclosed by a plain wooden fence. In 1897, two families who were on their way to the Klondike, the Cards and the McKays, lost infants to illness while camped at Lindeman Lake and buried them side by side before continuing on. If either of those tiny coffins is buried here, there is no longer any indication. All the wooden markers are either lying facedown or weathered beyond legibility. The Cards' seven-month-old baby, their first child, was laid to rest holding a bunch of artificial violets that had been removed from a woman's hat. A few stampeders who came by later may have taken the time to gather flowers and place them on these graves. Now that is no longer necessary, since the burial mounds are adorned year-round by kinnikinnick, crowberry and bunchberry.

Every step along the trail, the past is with us.

Lindeman City to Bennett

Today we rise early, at least by our recent standards, but we are put to shame by two men and a boy who show up as we are eating breakfast in front of the cabin. It is only 8:45 a.m. and they have already come the 8.8 kilometres from Happy Camp. The boy's father has the haircut, muscle bulk and bearing of a military man, and appears to be the one in charge of this group. He tells us they are aiming to reach Log Cabin, out on the highway, this afternoon. By taking the cutoff trail at Bare Loon Lake and bypassing Bennett they will have managed to complete the trail in only two and a half days. Although the father is carrying his 10-year-old son's gear as well as his own, the boy has the dazed look of a new recruit halfway through boot camp.

At first I think their pace is to blame, but when they pull out their provisions, I revise this impression and decide his condition might have something to do with the food. Mark and I and a couple from New Jersey with whom we are sharing the table watch amazed as they cut open several flat foil pouches, pour cold water into them, and a few minutes later start spooning steaming food into their mouths.

"What is that?" I ask.

"Spanish omelette," one of the men answers between mouthfuls. He opens another package and pulls out a thin, beige rectangle. "Toast," he says, and takes a bite.

St. Andrew's Church, Bennett, where many offered prayers of thanks — and more than a few mourned fellow travellers.

It requires several minutes of further questioning to establish that they are consuming Meals Ready to Eat, or MRES in the lingo of the U.S. Army — no cooking required due to some magic of chemical reactions that take place in the lining of the foil pouches. They don't seem entirely clear — or particularly concerned — about how it works. The food tastes good, they assure us, but in case anyone should crave more flavour, Uncle Sam has provided some genuine Tabasco sauce to go along with this MRE. The soldier holds up a six-centimetre-high bottle, an exact replica of the larger bottle sitting in our fridge at home.

"I'm not going to use it," he says. "You can have it if you want."

"Sure," I reply and take it from him. My Chilkoot souvenir.

When they are done eating they restow their gear, swing their packs onto their shoulders, and stride off back toward the main trail. Total time elapsed since their arrival: 35 minutes. We all shake our heads. Then we return to the conversation we had been having earlier about the aurora borealis that shimmered overhead last night and other highlights of this hike. The folks from New Jersey both agree it has been well worth coming this far to experience the Chilkoot. Eventually, when we have finished the last dregs of our coffee, we all admit that perhaps it is time to get on our way. There is no need for long farewells. We know we will see each other at Bennett and probably en route, too.

This is the start of our seventh day on the trail. The routine of striking camp has become quick and easy. As I pack, I dream about wandering like this for a fortnight or a month. I am not eager to return home to the pressures of work and the neurotic pace of urban life. One fantasy leads to another, and soon I'm figuring out how we could come back next summer and complete the second half of the Klondike odyssey — the journey by water up to Dawson. Ever since the Whitehorse Rapids were dammed in 1957 it has been impossible to exactly replicate the stampeders' Yukon River adventures, but I would be willing to settle for a reasonable facsimile.

My mind is half on future possibilities and half on present realities as we begin the final leg of this trip. There is no need to hurry, since the distance from Lindeman to Bennett is just over 11 kilometres. Immediately east of the campground, we cross a high bridge over Moose Creek and begin to climb a long, gradual hill. Yesterday there was a slight haze in the air from the smoke of a distant forest fire. Today the air is clear and we are treated to superb views of Lindeman Lake. The trail tops out on a rocky knoll, then winds along through an open forest of scrubby pines. We pass a few small lakes and look hopefully for moose along their margins, but with no success.

While we are eating lunch beside Dan Johnson Lake, I hear chittering overhead. The birds making these dry, hoarse-sounding notes are moving fitfully among the treetops, and it takes me a few minutes to focus on them with my binoculars long enough to identify them as white-winged crossbills, year-round inhabitants of the boreal forest. They are too far away for me to see their

A shortcut for the brave — or the foolhardy. Being neither, we opt for the land route.

overlapping mandibles, which they are using to extract seeds from the spruce cones, but both the rosy-coloured males and the olive-grey females bear the species' distinctive white wing bars.

A short distance beyond our lunch and bird-watching stop we come to the Bare Loon Lake campground. I remember being drenched with sweat the last time I arrived here and gratefully diving into the lake's cool waters. Swimming is a less enticing prospect today; although the sun is shining, there is a cool breeze blowing.

A woman is sitting beside the trail with clipboards and papers, a graduate student conducting a trail-user survey as part of her master's thesis research. We stop to fill out her questionnaire and chat with her about her study. When she mentions that she has been at Bare Loon Lake every day distributing surveys, I ask if she has seen anyone who meets Adrian's description. "You must mean the photographer," she replies immediately. "He came through yesterday and we talked for a few minutes, but he sure was in a hurry to get to the end of the trail." I guess we won't be catching up to him, but at least we now have some idea how he has fared since disappearing down the trail with his wet sleeping bag.

A sign on the north side of Bare Loon Lake indicates the cutoff trail to the right. From this junction it is about two kilometres to the railway line, then another eight kilometres along the tracks back to where the railway and the highway intersect. We continue straight ahead, still paralleling Lindeman Lake. Along the way we pass a trapping cabin that belongs to members of the Carcross-Tagish First Nation, who have retained aboriginal subsistence rights within the boundaries of Chilkoot Trail National Historic Site.

One doesn't expect a 53-kilometre trail that begins in the rainforest to end up in the desert, but that is more or less what happens on the Chilkoot. Around the cabin there are trees but little ground cover other than kinnikinnick. As we go farther north, the kinnikinnick becomes increasingly sparse and instead of rocks underfoot we suddenly find ourselves hiking across gritty, yellow sand that drags at our every step. Widely spaced pines scattered across the dunes give the scene a surreal quality, as if it had been conjured up by a child who thought that the Magi crossing the desert with their gifts should have a few Christmas trees around to signify the purpose of their journey.

Although not visible from the trail, Lindeman Creek is running along to our left as we hike across the sand dunes. The creek, which flows from Lindeman Lake into Bennett Lake, was sometimes referred to by the stampeders as One Mile River, despite being only about a kilometre long. Shallow and boulder-strewn — "a nasty thoroughfare," in the words of Tappan Adney — it was a navigational hazard for those who built their boats at Lindeman City. The Tlingits had generally portaged between the lakes, as indicated by their name for the place, Ch'akhúxh Anaxh Duǂ.adi Yé, meaning "place for packing skin boats over." But the stampeders' massive wooden skiffs and scows were not made to be carried.

Overnight a tent city sprang up on the shores of Lindeman Creek and Lake Bennett.
Boats were hurriedly built as spring thaw approached.

While many played it safe by attaching ropes to their boats and easing them down this stretch of river from the safety of the shore, Adney and his partner were more daring. One standing at the bow and one at the stern, each wielding an oar, they flew through the white water without getting so much as a scratch on their brand-new dory.

Twenty-six-year-old John Matthews, who tried twice to shoot these same rapids, was not so lucky. On his first attempt he wrecked his boat and lost his entire outfit. Undaunted, he returned a short time later with another boat and a new outfit. Instead of learning from his previous mistakes and taking a different approach, he tried again to run the rapids fully loaded and once more he failed. The loss proved too much for the young man. Standing on the shore beside his second wrecked boat and the remnants of his second ruined outfit, he pulled out a gun and killed himself before anyone could stop him. Those who had seen this tragedy unfold buried him where he lay. I have heard that if you walk up the river from Bennett, Matthews's grave can still be found.

In the early days of the gold rush, hardly any stampeders considered going all the way to Bennett Lake to build their boats. As far as they were concerned, Lindeman City was the northern terminus of the Chilkoot Trail. Many later arrivals took one look at Lindeman Creek and the diminishing supply of timber at the south end of Lindeman Lake, and carried on north to where the town of

Bennett was taking shape. Bennett's growth was also fed by the influx of stampeders arriving via the White Pass Trail, which joined the Chilkoot route at the foot of Lindeman Lake. By late winter in 1898, thousands of tents had been pitched at the head of Bennett Lake and all the way back up Lindeman Creek. The usual assortment of hotels, eateries and stores had also appeared, many of them housed in log cabins and frame buildings. Bennett's peak population, just before breakup in the spring of 1898, may have been as high as 20,000.

The main activity for the majority of these people was boat-building. The sounds of sawing and hammering rang through the town. One far-seeing individual had already established a sawmill at Bennett before the stampede began, and five more began churning out lumber for eager buyers as the rush picked up speed. The tension in Bennett throughout May 1898 must have been incredible. Spring was in the air, but ice still locked the lake. Almost everybody was waiting for the moment when it would break and they could begin the race to Dawson. Finally, on May 29, the ice started moving, and within 48 hours the lake was open. Thousands of boats — some say more than 7,000 — were launched in the last two days of the month. The wind gave them a bit of a push on the first morning, then died, leaving a multitude of becalmed vessels covering the water like leaves on a pond. Some people took out oars or paddles and made what progress they could; others floated and waited. The moment a breeze sprang up, sails were raised and Bennett Lake came alive as boats of every description all headed north.

To me this is the second most compelling image of the stampede, rivalled only by the image of the endless line of people climbing the Golden Stairs. I replay the scene in my mind as I slog across the sand. We are climbing now, just enough to slow our progress and make me feel impatient to get to the top of this rise and see the lake. It's about 2:00 p.m., four hours since we left Lindeman City, when I catch sight of our New Jersey breakfast companions standing on a rocky outcrop a short distance ahead and know that we have reached the lookout I've been eagerly anticipating.

When we get there, the view is as beautiful and as powerful as I remember. The broad band of blue-green water is framed by mountains that sweep skyward directly from the shore, cradling the lake in a wide V. In the distance, the mountains draw the water ever closer into their embrace until it seems the lake has disappeared or slipped through them into some other, mysterious land. I imagine what it would have been like to stand here as the boats pulled away from the shore, their sails billowing, and to watch them shrink in the distance and vanish. A myriad of dreamers racing toward their destiny. Today there is only a small flotilla of black ducks bobbing on the pewter waves.

After we leave the viewpoint it takes only a few more minutes to reach Bennett. Unlike the other Chilkoot ghost towns, this one has buildings, although the church is the only surviving vestige from before the turn of the century. Of all the boom-and-bust towns along the Chilkoot Trail, except Dyea, Bennett had the longest life span. As the head of navigation on the Yukon River system, it attracted a number of steamboat companies, which built wharves and warehouses along the waterfront and kept nearly a dozen paddle wheelers moving back and forth between Bennett and Miles Canyon, near Whitehorse. Throughout 1898 and 1899, wooden buildings increasingly took the place of tents. When St. Andrew's Presbyterian Church was completed in the summer of 1899, its handsome steeple added a reassuring touch of permanence to the skyline, but that illusion was soon to be shattered by the White Pass and Yukon Route railway. When the tracks first reached Bennett on July 6, 1899, the railway breathed fresh life into Bennett, reinforcing its importance as a transfer point for Klondike-bound freight and passengers. Just 12 months later, however, the last spike was driven on the second phase of the line, which now extended all the way to Whitehorse. Bennett's entire reason for existence was eliminated. By 1902, the town was deserted.

Evidence of the past is everywhere around the townsite. Terracing on the hillside below the church indicates where tents and buildings once stood. Elsewhere the faint outlines of old foundations can be seen. The sparse ground cover vegetation here, like that at Lindeman City, makes artifacts easy to see, and it is impossible to walk 20 paces without coming across a rusty tin can or a fragment of old glass. The most interesting items are undoubtedly long gone, but Parks Canada archaeologists have still managed to expand their knowledge of the town by examining what has been left. The preponderance of champagne bottles dumped behind the Klondyke Hotel, for example, offers some insights into the drinking habits of the stampeders who frequented its bar. One theory is that all drinks were sold for the same exorbitant price because of the cost of transportation: there was no reason to order beer when you could be living it up with champagne.

We pitch our tent on one of the lakeside terraces, then walk up Lindeman Creek to get water. I have no desire to drink from the lake immediately in front of the camping area, since it is a popular place for bathing and I have noticed some people using copious amounts of soap. After we return with our full water bottles, we go back up the hill to have a better look at the church. The doors are locked and the windows boarded up, but it is the exterior, with its rustic siding of barked slabs from the Bennett sawmills, that is of most interest. To make up for the simplicity of their materials, the workmen who built this church took care to arrange these slabs in a decorative manner.

From the church, we continue east over to the railway station, which dates back to the early 1900s, then return to camp via a set of interpretive panels explaining the relationship between local First Nations people and the land. Not far from the exhibit is a residence belonging to a Carcross-Tagish family that traces its use of the Bennett Lake area to the beginning of this century. This lake, known to the Tagish as Men Cho ("big lake"), is part of their ancestral territory, which covered more than 10,000 square kilometres. Traditionally, the Tagish followed a seasonal round of hunting, fishing, trapping and berry picking. This lifestyle was severely compromised during the Klondike gold rush, as hordes of gold seekers thundered through their territory, disrupting their society and clearing large sections of forest.

After the stampede the damaged habitat gradually healed, but there had been too many other changes for the First Nations to completely reclaim their old ways. Since it was no longer possible for them to move about and live off the land as freely as they had in the past, many families built cabins in strategic locations and used them as a base. Bennett proved to be well situated for the family that settled here. In springtime, the hill east of the train station was a prime location for getting ptarmigan, and throughout the summer, Bennett and Lindeman lakes yielded whitefish, trout and grayling. In August and September the women and children harvested low-bush cranberries, mossberries and blueberries. Fall was the main time for hunting moose and caribou. Winter was trapping season.

For many years, local hunters provided the White Pass and Yukon Route railway with fresh meat, and passengers were treated to moose or caribou stew when the train made its regular lunch stop at Bennett. I wouldn't mind a nice bowl of moose stew for dinner tonight, but we have to be content with the last of our freeze-dried meals. Unlike the others we have eaten on this trip, it is not inspiring.

Happily, morning brings a culinary experience we have been looking forward to ever since we heard about it back in Skagway. As a special Klondike gold-rush centennial event, the Yukon Outdoors Club has set up the Chilkoot Sourdough Bakery at the Bennett campground. Using ingredients donated by a long list of sponsors, volunteers from the club have spent the summer serving free sour-dough hotcakes to hikers every morning. By 8:00 a.m., when the bakery is due to open, a long line of hungry campers clutching plates, cups and cutlery has formed outside the bakery tent. Right on schedule, the door opens and a woman in a long Victorian dress steps out, coffee pot in hand. Another similarly attired woman appears at a serving window and starts dishing out hotcakes. I learn later, when the feeding frenzy is over, that our hostesses are Judy Dabbs and Pat McKenna, two-thirds of the trio of women who dreamed up this idea. Judy is the great-grandniece of William Ogilvie, who was the Yukon territorial commissioner during the gold rush. The third member of the group, Ione Christensen, also traces her northern roots back to the gold rush.

Ione's special contribution to this undertaking was providing the starter for the sourdough hotcakes. Sourdough, a fermented dough used instead of yeast as leavening for baked goods, is a venerable northern tradition. A small amount of dough is saved from each batch of bread to act as a starter for the next batch. Amazingly, the sourdough starter that went into the hotcakes being served up this morning is a direct descendant of the starter that was carried over the Chilkoot Pass in 1898 by Ione's great-grandfather, Wesley Ballentine, and his

Bennett Lake may mark the end of the Chilkoot Trail, but fortune seekers still had many a mile to go to the Klondike.

sons. Over the past 100 years it has been passed down through Ione's family from generation to generation.

We enjoy our hotcakes and coffee in the company of our friends from New Jersey, while Judy and Pat work tirelessly for nearly an hour and a half until at last everyone has had their fill. Then the cooks and their children, also in costume, begin cleaning up. Although their stint out here has already lasted a couple of weeks, they are still cheerful and enthusiastic. Judy says that by the time they shut down, one week from now, she and the other volunteers will have flipped about 15,000 hotcakes and fed well over 2,000 backpackers.

After breakfast we pack up, one eye on the dark clouds overhead. Then we walk over to the railway station to stow our packs and join the Parks Canada interpretive tour that fills the hour before the train's scheduled departure. There is a good crowd assembled for the tour, a mix of people like us who have just come off the trail, backpackers who are about to hike it in the reverse direction and people who have just come up on the train for the day. Our guide, Roseanne Konrad, leads us through the town, pointing out where various buildings once stood, showing us historical photographs and telling stories about the gold rush and Bennett.

While we are standing near the original location of the North-West Mounted Police detachment headquarters, she mentions that one of the men died here and was interred in the Bennett cemetery. My ears perk up. I had failed to realize there was a burial ground here, despite my cemetery fixation (which I attribute to my parents, who tended to take me to old graveyards instead of more traditional spots, like amusement parks, when I was a child). On our way to the church, the last stop on the tour, I ask Roseanne about the cemetery, and she tells me it is 15 minutes back up the trail. Although the train is due to leave in about half an hour, I am consumed with a desire to visit these last Chilkoot graves. Mark, who shares my fixation, agrees to come with me.

Off we go, charging down the trail in the rain that has just started to fall. After five minutes of running on the soft sand, we are both panting. We slow down a little, afraid of going right past the cemetery without seeing it, as we did on the way into Bennett. I am almost ready to give up and turn back when I spot some fenced plots on a low ridge a few hundred metres east of the trail. When we get up there we find about 20 graves, only a few of which have legible markers. While Mark takes some pictures, I make a few quick notes. Then we hurry back to Bennett. By the time we reach the station, the rain is pelting down. We load our packs onto the open baggage car, find seats for ourselves in one of the passenger cars, and peel off our wet raincoats as the train starts to pull slowly out of the station, swaying gently on its narrow rails. Then I open my notebook and reread the words I have just copied down:

At rest
But not forgotten
Laughlen McLean
Age 62 years
Died May 14th 1898
Leaves wife & family
at Richmond
P. Quebec Canada

Laughlen McLean — just one of the tens of thousands who came this way a century ago. In the years since the Chilkoot was revived as a recreational trail, close to 50,000 more people have walked the distance from Dyea to Bennett. And all of us, stampeders and modern backpackers alike, have been following in the footsteps of First Nations people who discovered this passage from the coast to the interior so far back in time that only the rocks remember the beginning.

Many made the trip to the Klondike, but some fell short of the end of the rainbow.

Epilogue: Return to Skagway

IN THE EARLY DAYS OF THE KLONDIKE GOLD RUSH, THERE WAS A GREAT RIVALRY among advocates of the various routes to Dawson, with the fiercest competition being between the promoters of the Chilkoot and White Pass Trails. The Chilkoot was the shorter of the two, by 14 kilometres, but the White Pass offered easier grades. The Chilkoot Pass was a particularly intimidating prospect. Nevertheless, after taking into account all they had heard, and in some cases hiking both trails for a firsthand assessment, most stampeders decided on the shorter route. During the winter of 1897-98, an estimated 5,000 to 10,000 people transported their outfits over the White Pass, compared to the 25,000 to 30,000 who favoured the Chilkoot.

Meanwhile, a small group of men who had no intention of going to Dawson and digging for gold were eyeing the two trails with a view to establishing a railway to the interior, for as every smart Victorian capitalist knew, only the steam locomotive could propel North America toward the prosperous future that was its rightful destiny. Both routes presented daunting obstacles to railway construction, but in April 1898, a Canadian engineer named Michael Heney identified a viable course up the Skagway Valley and over the White Pass. Soon afterwards, Heney chanced to meet a trio of British investors in Skagway who were there to investigate the feasibility of building a railroad. A deal was quickly struck, and by the end of May, construction had begun on the newly created White Pass and Yukon Route railway.

The easy way out: the White Pass and Yukon railway returns the traveler to tidewater.

Of the three possibilities for returning from Bennett to civilization at the end of a Chilkoot backpacking trip — on foot to the highway, by boat to Carcross or by train to Fraser or Skagway — I think the latter provides the most satisfying finale, though I have to admit I haven't tried the boat option yet. Taking the train all the way to Skagway gives hikers a chance to compare the White Pass Trail to the one they have just completed and to see the engineering marvel that rang the death knell for the Chilkoot.

The trip is also a treat for anyone who likes old trains. Most of the WP&YR's passenger cars are either originals that have been refurbished or new stock built to vintage specifications. The names painted on the sides of the cars commemorate the region's lakes: Klukshu, Fairweather, Homan, Nares and others. Diesel-electric locomotives do the bulk of the work and the single surviving steam engine is only put into service on special occasions, but a vintage red caboose is usually present to add a pleasing, authentic touch.

The WP&YR is a narrow-gauge railway with tracks set slightly less than one metre apart. One reason its builders chose this design is that the smaller turning radius of the narrow tracks made it easier for trains to negotiate the serpentine route up the Skagway Valley, which includes curves as tight as 16 degrees. The second reason is that a three-metre-wide roadbed (compared to the conventional 4.5 metres) meant less rock had to be blasted. Even so, workers used 450 tons of explosives to carve out the roadbed from Skagway to the White Pass summit.

The 20-kilometre stretch between Bennett and Fraser is almost completely level. Rattling south from Fraser, after the train has dropped off some passengers and picked up others, I begin to appreciate why the WP&YR has been declared an

International Historic Civil Engineering Landmark, one of only 20 in the world. This is one of the steepest railroads in North America, gaining 873 metres in 32 kilometres, with grades of up to 3.9 percent. A short distance below the summit is a steel bridge that was the world's tallest cantilever when it was completed in 1901. Before it was built, the trains followed a dizzying series of switchbacks up and down this slope. In places farther down the line, the tracks cling to sheer rock walls. To construct these sections, the workers hung suspended by ropes from cliffs hundreds of metres high, blasting, chipping and drilling. Not only is this section of the line an amazing feat of engineering and construction, it was completed in record time, despite winter blizzards, bone-chilling temperatures and the defection of numerous workers every time rumours of a new gold rush hit town.

Many stampeders who slogged over the Chilkoot Trail in 1897 or 1898 would have made their first trip back "outside" via the WP&YR. What a revelation it must have been for them to travel so effortlessly after all the hardships and worries of their incoming journey. I feel it myself, though I was only on the trail for a week and did not have a ton of goods to move from one end to the other. Near Fraser, the rocky, windswept plateau is reminiscent of the high alpine country around Happy Camp and Deep Lake. Winding down the valley toward the ocean, the trees gradually become taller and the rainforest reasserts itself. There's the devil's club that I last saw at Sheep Camp. There are the ferns that lined the trail on the way to Finnegan's Point.

One and a half hours after leaving Fraser station, we roll into Skagway. The streets are teeming with people, just as they were a week ago, and, as usual in summer, several colossal white cruise ships are tied up at the long wharves. Unlike Dyea, which slipped into oblivion when the railway upstaged the Chilkoot Trail, Skagway gained influence as a critical transfer point for freight and passengers travelling to and from the northern interior. Although Skagway's population declined from more than 8,000 in the spring of 1898 to fewer than 1,000 in 1910, the town endured, partly because of tourism. The first sightseers arrived during the stampede. Their numbers increased through the following decades, declined during World War II, then picked up again in the 1950s. These days visitors inundate Skagway from May to September.

Walking up Broadway from the train station, past stores that specialize in diamonds and emeralds, T-shirts and postcards, gold-nugget jewelry and Swiss watches, ice cream and popcorn, Irish linens and Russian trinkets, I am struck by how little Skagway has changed in one hundred years. It is still a gold-rush town — drawing its wealth from tourists now, instead of stampeders — and, in its own way, it is as much a part of the Chilkoot experience as the serene shores of Lindeman Lake. We've come full circle. Our journey is complete.

Logistics for the Modern Stampeder

WHEN NEWS OF THE KLONDIKE GOLD DISCOVERY REACHED THE OUTSIDE WORLD in July 1897, thousands of people made spur-of-the-moment decisions to journey north and seek their fortunes. Based on little more than rumours and third-hand information, many of them chose the Chilkoot Trail as their route to the goldfields. Men and women who had spent their lives in offices and parlours declared their intentions to rush headlong into the wilderness. They bought food, clothing and equipment with little or no knowledge of the conditions they would face. They booked passage on steamers bound for a town they had never even heard of one week earlier, and, without further ado, they kissed their loved ones good-bye. It's a wonder most of them survived.

One hundred years after the Klondike stampede, there is no excuse for tackling the Chilkoot Trail unprepared. This appendix provides a starting point for planning your trip. Many bookstores and libraries carry a selection of backpacking primers. Most major cities have a reputable outdoor equipment store where all the basic or deluxe gear the modern hiker requires or desires can be purchased. Parks Canada and the U.S. National Park Service provide a comprehensive trail information package, including an excellent map. Train, bus and ferry information is just a phone call or an Internet connection away. I've listed some costs (in Canadian dollars unless otherwise indicated), but these, as well as schedules, are subject to change and should be confirmed before setting out.

On Chilkoot Pass

The first question when considering a Chilkoot trip is when to go. Originally, the main use of this trail was as a winter/spring travel route. Each year in midwinter, the Tlingits crossed the mountains to meet with their trading partners in the interior and make arrangements for the spring trading season. In April, they made another journey over the pass, returning home a few weeks later laden with winter furs. The advent of the Klondike gold rush turned the Chilkoot into a year-round route. Today the main hiking season is from late May to early September. The trail remains open during the other two-thirds of the year, but there are no park personnel patrolling and marking the route during these months.

Those who would consider hiking the Chilkoot in winter should bear in mind that temperatures can drop as low as minus 45 degrees Celsius. Factor in wind speeds of up to 100 kilometres per hour and I start shivering just thinking about it. Precipitation is heavy and comes in all forms, depending upon proximity to the coast and time of year. It is common for blowing snow or driving sleet and rain to reduce visibility to less than eight metres. Up around the pass, the snow reaches depths of five to 10 metres. Spring thaw brings an extreme avalanche hazard. In short, travelling outside the main hiking season is difficult and risky.

Although generations of experience made the Tlingits and the Tagish intimately familiar with the land and the weather, First Nations travellers occasionally suffered injury or death. The fact that so many stampeders success-fully negotiated the Chilkoot route in winter, despite their general lack of knowledge or preparation, was mainly because of their sheer numbers. The steady stream of people supplied customers for a profusion of eating and sleeping establishments, and support for anyone who might run into trouble. The constant movement of humans and pack animals up and down the trail kept the snow tramped down and the route clearly defined. The ascent of the pass was merely a matter of climbing the steps that had been carved out of the snow. It was tiring, but a lot easier than tackling this steep slope on snowshoes or skis.

These days, the trail is not busy between September and May. The number of people making the trip in late spring and summer, on the other hand, is steadily increasing. A few years ago, Parks Canada and the U.S. National Park Service agreed to restrict the number of Chilkoot backpackers crossing the pass to 50 per day. This is the part of the trail that is most susceptible to overcrowding, because almost everyone makes Sheep Camp their departure point and Happy Camp their destination on the day they scale the pass.

Of the 50 trip permits issued for each day, 42 can be reserved in advance and eight are held for walk-ins. These are offered on a first-come, first-served basis at the Trail Center in Skagway (on Broadway at 2nd Avenue) the day before departure. Reserved trip permits must be picked up from the Trail Center by noon on the day the trip begins. Any unclaimed permits are treated as cancellations and are added to the walk-in allocation. The maximum allowable group size is 12, and only one group of more than nine people is allowed per day.

Reservations cost an extra $10 on top of the permit fee. They are highly recommended for midsummer trips unless you have the time and money to hang around Skagway for several days, reporting to the Trail Center each afternoon at 1:00 p.m. to take your chances on securing a permit. Reservations can be made by contacting the Parks Canada office in Whitehorse at 1-800-661-0486 if you are calling from Canada or the United States, or (867) 667-3910 from overseas. Reservations are accepted up to two years in advance. Most summer and many spring openings are booked by the end of the previous March. If you decide to cancel your trip, the reservation and permit fees are nonrefundable. You are, however, allowed a single change to your booking, provided alternative dates are available.

Overnight trip permits cost $35 for adults and $17.50 for children from six to 15 years old. Day permits, required on the Canadian side only, cost $5 for adults and $2.50 for children. Chilkoot Trail permit fees were introduced by Parks Canada in 1997 in an effort to offset the costs of trail and facility maintenance and information services. By mutual agreement, none of the money goes to the U.S. Park Service, as they have a no-fee policy. If you stay on the American side you require a backcountry permit for overnight trips, but this is provided for free.

Although there is no procedure for systematic inspection of permits, wardens and rangers are entitled to make random checks, and anyone who can't show the right paperwork may be fined. Crossing the pass on a date other than your designated summit day is the misdemeanour most likely to get you into trouble. I heard of one man who was unable to get the date he wanted and decided to go anyway, one day ahead of schedule. Another party reported him to a warden, who checked his permit when he reached the summit and turned him back to Sheep Camp.

Whether you reserve your place on the trail in advance or pick up a permit the day before you start hiking, be prepared to provide a firm itinerary. Your summit day is the most critical date, but you will also be required to say where you will camp each night. These requirements annoy some people, who feel this kind of regimentation has no place in the wilderness. The reality, however, is that popular trails like the Chilkoot can only retain their environmental integrity by having designated campgrounds and limiting the number of campers. Subalpine sites like Happy Camp are particularly vulnerable to overuse and are the slowest to recover from abuse.

Of course, planning an itinerary should be part of your preparation for any backpacking trip, so, regardless of the demands of the permit system, you will need to decide how far to hike each day and where to camp at night. The answer depends on your objectives. Do you simply want to get from one end of the trail to the other in the shortest time possible or do you hope to enjoy some sight-seeing? Be sure to factor in the abilities of the weakest member of your party. The largest and most heavily used campgrounds are Sheep Camp (81 campers maximum), Lindeman City (60), Canyon City (60) and Happy Camp (50). Lake Bennett and Bare Loon Lake, which both accommodate approximately 30 people, are also popular. Those who enjoy solitude are most likely to find it at Finnegan's Point, Pleasant Camp or Deep Lake, where the occupancy limits are 15, 27 and 20 campers, respectively.

During the Klondike gold rush, many stampeders spent months along the Chilkoot route, moving their supplies and gear stage by stage from tidewater at Dyea, over the pass, and down to Bennett. In the modern era, athletic enthusiasts run this entire distance in a day, most of them trying to meet or match the record of approximately eight hours. The majority of backpackers fall somewhere in between these two extremes, hiking the trail over a three- to five-day period.

On my first Chilkoot trip I spent five nights on the trail. The second time, researching this book was my main goal, and I stayed out for seven and a half days. Doing the trip in three days is fine if you are fit enough and that's all the time you have available, but for most hikers I think slower is better. Not only does a relaxed pace reduce the potential pain and strain, it also allows you to

Not all the trail is a tough uphill slog

look around and really see all that the trail has to offer. Less experienced hikers who are considering tackling the Chilkoot should do at least one weekend excursion with full packs beforehand to get a sense of their capabilities. Some sort of physical training to prepare your heart, lungs and muscles for the trip is also highly recommended.

For most backpackers, direction of travel over the Chilkoot route is not an issue. They want to follow in the stampeders' footsteps, starting at the coast and ending at the headwaters of the Yukon River. There are also three good practical reasons why at least 96 percent of all Chilkoot trekkers go from south to north. First of all, it's easier and safer. Climbing up the Golden Stairs is more of a cardiovascular workout, but descending this rocky slope places a much greater strain on knees and ankles, and is more treacherous, especially in wet, windy or foggy conditions. The timing of travel over the pass is also better for north-bound hikers. Departing from Sheep Camp, you have the hardest part of the day behind you once you reach the summit. Travelling in the opposite direction, you end up negotiating the Golden Stairs later in the day, instead of when you are freshest. The third reason is the weather. Almost all summer storms flow inland from the Pacific Ocean, blowing up the valley and over the mountains in a northerly direction. Therefore, no matter how bad it gets, if you're heading north you can nearly always count on the wind and rain being at your back. This is an important consideration for the one-third of the trail that is above the treeline and fully exposed to the elements.

Before you finalize your trip itinerary, you will also need to consider your options for getting to and from the trail. By car or bus, Skagway is a scenic 176-kilometre drive from Whitehorse on a paved road known as the Klondike Highway. Otherwise, access is by sea or by air. The Alaska Marine Highway System, 1-800-642-0066, runs ferries from Bellingham, Washington, and Prince Rupert, British Columbia, up the Inside Passage to Skagway and Haines. Three local airlines fly daily between Juneau and Skagway.

If you are not taking your own vehicle to Skagway, a number of local operators run shuttle buses or taxis to the trailhead at Dyea: Chilkat Guides, (907) 983-2627; Frontier Excursions, (907) 983-2512; Skagway Float Tours, (907) 983-3508; Dyea Dave, (907) 983-2731. In 1998, the going rate for this 16-kilometre trip was U.S.$10 per person. It is legal to hitchhike, but there is little traffic on the Skagway-Dyea road.

At the north end of the trail, travellers bound for Whitehorse may wish to follow the gold-rush route a little farther beyond the end of the trail by taking a boat up Bennett Lake to the Yukon village of Carcross. Chilkoot Water Charters, (867) 821-3209 or (867) 821-4416, and Bennett Charters, (867) 667-1486, offered this service in 1998 for $50 per person. There is no phone at Bennett, so pickup must be prearranged.

The closest road access to Bennett is at Log Cabin, 13 kilometres as the train rolls or 10 kilometres along the cutoff trail from Bare Loon Lake. Hiking out to Log Cabin is the least expensive way to return to civilization but has the disadvantage of being a somewhat anticlimactic denouement, since the cutoff trail is not particularly scenic. During the gold rush, Log Cabin was the last staging point before Bennett on the White Pass Trail — the site of a typical stampede community and a North-West Mounted Police post. Now it is a parking lot beside the highway. There is no telephone, so if you want to get picked up there you will need to make arrangements before starting your hike. The various Skagway shuttle services charge about U.S.$20 to $25 per person for transport between Log Cabin and Skagway. The cost is about the same if you are heading north to Whitehorse. Alaska Direct, 1-800-770-6652, and the WP&YR, 1-800-343-7373, both operate a daily bus service between Whitehorse and Skagway. Stops at Log Cabin or Fraser should be prearranged.

The third, and most popular, way of leaving Bennett is by rail. Depending upon your budget and your final destination, you can go all the way back to Skagway or get off at Fraser, eight kilometres south of Log Cabin. It should be noted that Fraser consists of nothing more than a Canada Customs post and a

A century's trekkers have added to trail-marking cairns

railway platform. There is no public telephone. The White Pass and Yukon Route's hiker service runs five days a week (every day except Tuesday and Wednesday). Trains depart from Bennett station at 9:00 a.m. and 1:00 p.m. The advance fare from Bennett to Fraser is U.S.$25 for all riders. From Bennett to Skagway it is U.S.$65 for adults and half-price for children. Tickets purchased on the train cost an extra U.S.$15. Call the WP&YR at 1-800-343-7373 to make reservations or confirm fares and schedules, or check their Web site at www.whitepassrailroad.com.

However you decide to make your entrances and exits, at some point you will need to deal with the fact that in crossing the Chilkoot Pass you have also crossed an international border. Hikers who travel from south to north are required to clear Canadian customs at Fraser or Whitehorse as soon as possible after coming off the trail. Those who make the trek in the opposite direction must register with U.S. Customs at the National Park Service Information Center, across from the Trail Center in Skagway. Make sure you have appropriate identification with you.

Accommodations in Skagway are almost all high-priced and often fully booked. The least expensive option is the Home Hostel, (907) 983-2131. For the best historic atmosphere, try one of the heritage hotels that began operating

during the stampede. Names and contact information can be obtained from the Skagway Convention and Visitors Bureau, (907) 983-2854 or www.skagway.org.

Once you have figured out your travel plans, both on and off the trail, you can turn your thoughts to packing. First, get on the bathroom scale and see how much you weigh. Calculate 30 percent of that number. This is the maximum amount your pack should weigh. Although you might be able to get away with carrying more than the recommended load, your enjoyment of the trip will be inversely proportional to the excess weight in your pack.

Essentials for the trip include the following: a lightweight tent with full-sized rain fly; a cold-weather sleeping bag and insulated sleeping pad; a backpacking stove; matches in a waterproof container; enough fuel and food (including plenty of quick-energy snacks) for the planned duration of your trip, plus one extra day in case of emergency; as few cooking and eating utensils as you can get by with; a pocket knife; sturdy, comfortable, well-broken-in and waterproofed hiking boots; an extra change of socks; durable rain pants and a good-quality rain jacket (which can double as a windbreaker); a waterproof pack cover and/or plastic bags for wrapping your clothing and sleeping bag to keep them dry; one set of hiking clothes, plus extras to change into if you get wet; a wool hat and gloves or mitts; several layers of warm outerwear; long underwear if you are susceptible to cold; a first-aid kit that includes blister treatments; a water bottle and some means of purifying your drinking water; nine metres of cord for hanging your food bag on bear poles; toilet paper; personal-care items like your toothbrush; sunscreen, sunglasses and a sunhat; a small flashlight; equipment repair kits; and a whistle for emergencies. You might want to add insect repellent, though I did not find the bugs too much of a problem — except at Finnegan's Point — either time I went over the Chilkoot, in early and mid-August.

If you still haven't reached your maximum weight allowance, I would highly recommend adding a pair of sandals or lightweight runners to wear around the campgrounds and give your feet some respite. Gaiters, which keep mud and snow out of your boots, are also a good idea, especially for early-season travel. In the realm of last-packed luxuries, I favour a good book, binoculars and a camera. If you are planning to travel back to civilization and hot showers by bus, it is considerate to take along one shirt that gets saved for your last day. The WP&YR spares the sensibilities of their nonhiker passengers, most of whom are off the cruise ships, by segregating the hikers in one train car. Nobody seems to mind, since it maintains the camaraderie of the trail until the last possible moment. Buses can't achieve this degree of separation. When I came off the trail in 1994 the bus driver asked all the hikers to sit at the back for the drive from Fraser to Whitehorse. There had been complaints in the past, he confided. We all willingly complied.

Notes on the Photography

WHEN THE FOLKS AT RAINCOAST ASKED ME TO TAKE ON AN ASSIGNMENT TO photograph the Chilkoot Trail for a book, I readily accepted. After all, it's not every day one gets invited to do one of the great classic hikes with someone else paying the bills. I was not so naive, however, as to think I was going on a holiday. I was made well aware of the formidable climb up the "Golden Stairs." And I would be obliged to carry, not only my camping gear, but photographic equipment as well.

I was also required to produce enough photographs to fill a book during a single week on the trail, a rather tall order considering that the time I had needed to do previous books was measured in years. The equipment I took, balancing weight versus need, would have to be considered carefully. In the end, I chose to bring with me a compact camera bag containing two fully manual 35 mm camera bodies, four lenses — a 24 mm, a 35 mm, a 50 mm and a 135mm — plus a Sekonic Studio Delux hand-held light meter for measuring incidental light.

My filters included two polarizers, one neutral density, a graduated neutral density, one intensifier and an 81c warming. Though I customarily use filters sparingly, I used all those I brought along at some point during the hike. On occasion I used two filters together: a warming filter to overcome the blue of the intensifier, and a neutral density with a polarizer in order to attain a slow enough shutter speed to create the smoky effect in moving water.

I also brought a very lightweight tripod that extends easily (a must when you're setting up a hundred times a day), a set of extension tubes and a soft cotton cloth for wiping lenses. (Never lens tissue.) Added to this were 30 rolls of film, most of which I carried in my pack. I used Fujichrome Velvia and Ektachrome 100s (Elite) exclusively. In most situations I have a slight preference for Velvia, although its disadvantage is having a slow 50 ISO rating. By the end of the trip I had exposed 23 rolls. Conspicuously absent from my bag were my 300 mm, my two-times converter, my 17 mm and my motor drive, all sacrificed to save weight.

The weather one cannot do anything about, of course. It was generally good except for being dreadful on the long slog between Sheep Camp and Happy Camp — high winds, fog and rain. All I can hope is that the photos taken that day reflect a little of the atmosphere that penetrated my bones, and presumably, that of the miners one hundred years earlier. The Chilkoot Trail is indeed a grunt, but an exhilarating one. Happy trails.

ADRIAN DORST

ARCHIVAL PHOTOGRAPHIC CREDITS

A rich archive of early Chilkoot Trail photography exists at the Special Collections Division of the University of Washington Libraries in Seattle. Black-and-white photographs in this books are reproduced with the Division's kind permission. Photographer's name and the negative number are listed below.

PAGE NO.

ii	(Winter & Pond, 337)
3	(Hegg, 54)
4	(Hegg, 97)
9	(Hegg, 85)
17	(La Roche, 2035)
21	(Hegg, 105)
28	(Hegg, 687)
35	(Hegg, 99)
39	(UW, 17586)
48	(UW, 18437)
50	(Hegg, 73a)
60	(UW, 579)
63	(Hegg, 214)
70	(Hegg, 669)
76	(UW, 18439)
101	(Hegg, 65)
114	(Cantrell, 46)

Further Reading

OTHER TRAVELLERS' TALES

Adney, Tappan. *The Klondike Stampede.* Vancouver: University of British Columbia Press, 1994.

Berry, Alice Edna. *The Bushes and the Berrys.* San Francisco: C. J. Bennett, 1978.

Black, Martha Louise. *My Ninety Years.* Anchorage: Alaska Northwest Publishing Company, 1976.

Craig, Lulu Alice. *Glimpses of Sunshine and Shade in the Far North.* Cincinnati: Editor Publishing Company, 1900.

Dawson, George M. *Report on an Exploration in the Yukon District, NWT, and Adjacent Northern Portions of British Columbia.* Whitehorse: Yukon Historical and Museum Association, 1987.

Oliver, Lillian Agnes. "My Klondike Mission," *Wide World Magazine,* April-September 1899, 43-54.

Reinicker, Juliette C., ed. *Klondike Letters: The Correspondence of a Gold Seeker in 1898.* Anchorage: Alaska Northwest Publishing Company, 1984. A collection of letters from Alfred McMichael.

Shape, William. *Faith of Fools: A Journal of the Klondike Gold Rush.* Seattle: Washington State University Press, 1998.

FIRST NATIONS HISTORY

Cruikshank, Julie. *Life Lived Like a Story: Life Stories of Three Yukon Native Elders.* Lincoln: University of Nebraska Press, 1990.

Emmons, George Thornton. *The Tlingit Indians.* Vancouver: Douglas and McIntyre, 1991.

Greer, Sheila. *Skookum Stories on the Chilkoot/Dyea Trail.* Carcross-Tagish First Nation, 1995.

McClellan, Catherine. *Part of the Land, Part of the Water: A History of the Yukon Indians.* Vancouver: Douglas and McIntyre, 1987.

FLORA, FAUNA AND GEOLOGY

Cannings, Richard, and Sydney Cannings. *British Columbia: A Natural History.* Vancouver: Douglas and McIntyre, 1996.

Connor, Cathy L., and Daniel O'Haire. *Roadside Geology of Alaska.* Missoula: Mountain Press, 1989.

MacKinnon, Andy, Jim Pojar, and Ray Coupé, eds. *Plants of Northern British Columbia.* Vancouver: Lone Pine Publishing, 1992.

Peterson, Roger Tory. *A Field Guide to Western Birds.* Boston: Houghton Mifflin Company, 1990.

Pojar, Jim, and Andy MacKinnon, eds. *Plants of Coastal British Columbia: Including Washington, Oregon and Alaska.* Vancouver: Lone Pine Publishing, 1994.

TRAIL GUIDES

Parks Canada and United States National Park Service. *A Hikers' Guide to the Chilkoot Trail.* Anchorage: Alaska Natural History Association, n.d. An annotated map.

Satterfield, Archie. *Chilkoot Pass: The Most Famous Trail in the North.* Anchorage: Alaska Northwest Publishing Company, 1983.

White-tailed ptarmigan.

Other titles in the Raincoast Journeys series:

Footsteps in the Clouds: Kangchenjunga a Century Later
by Baiba & Pat Morrow
ISBN 1-555192-226-6

Risking Adventure: Mountaineering Journeys Around the World
by Jim Haberl
1-55192-093-x

K2: Dreams and Reality
by Jim Haberl
1-55192-267-3

Haida Gwaii: Journeys Through the Queen Charlotte Islands
by Ian Gill & David Nunuk
1-55192-068-9

Western Journeys: Discovering the Secrets of the Land
by Daniel Wood & Beverley Sinclair
1-55192-069-7

Hiking on the Edge: West Coast Trail, Juan de Fuca Trail
by Ian Gill & David Nunuk
1-55192-146-4